Social Work and African-centred Worldviews

Mekada Graham

VENTURE PRESS

BASW website: http://www.basw.co.uk

Published by
VENTURE PRESS
16 Kent Street
Birmingham
B5 6RD

British Library Cataloguing-in-Publication Data
A catalogue record for this book is available from the British Library

ISBN   1 86178 049 4   (paperback)

Cover design by:
Western Arts
194 Goswell Road
London
EC1V 7DT

Printed in Great Britain

In the spirit of the ancestors I dedicate this book to mothers and fathers involved in collective endeavours to impart cultural resource knowledge to our children in order for them to know their purpose and to ensure their success in the world.

I give thanks and praises to all community-based organisations in Britain striving and thriving towards human excellence.

Contents   Page

Foreword

Mekada Graham, the winner of the 2000 Cheikh Anta Diop Award in Scholarship, has done as much as anyone to mould social work into a responsive field for multicultural societies. In *Social Work and African-centred Worldviews* she examines the plight of social work in Britain and critiques the various approaches to changing the life chances of victims of racism and domination. She understands more than most scholars that the fundamental problem of social work practice is not found in mere techniques but in the knowledge itself: that is, the source of the techniques and practices that pass as interventions. Her intellectual response to the current conditions in social work starts with the premise that most social work practice in Britain is founded on theories that have emerged from a unitary stream of thought, mainly Eurocentric, that does not take into consideration the present heterogeneity and multicultural state of British society.

What is clearly needed, and Graham lays it out quite boldly, is an innovation in social work thought that gets beyond the staid, old idea that you can use any technique designed for one set of clients for another set of clients without re-thinking the source of those ideas. This should not be seen as a revolutionary idea but, in reality, it is revolutionary when it questions the very ground upon which a field has built its entire corpus of interventions. The fact that social work was developed as it was in Britain, and in the USA, has a lot to do with the conception of the field during the past century when little thought was given to the nature of social work among those who were not white or European. Indeed, if there were a problem then it had to be solved using the same interventions that were used with whites. The idea might have been what was good for white people would be good for anybody else.

One of Mekada Graham's chief contributions is her work on the relationship between enslavement and the modern welfare state. She argues that there are four models of enslavement that have influenced the instruments of social welfare at a critical stage of development: (1) enslavement as a model of destitution, (2) enslavement as a model of social welfare, (3) enslavement as a model of salvation, and (4) enslavement as a model of social exclusion. Needless to say, Graham's construction is in effect a deconstruction of the way that the social welfare state has been looked at before. She shows precisely how the role of the African in the state impacted upon the way knowledge was developed and disseminated about social work. She writes, 'Ideologies of enslavement, whether pro or anti, were premised upon the notion that the

African was inferior, most often childlike, with a characteristic trait of absolute helplessness.' In the USA up until 1865 'enslavement was the major social welfare institution for African children'. Thus, in Britain and in the USA the social condition and welfare of the African was found in the enslavement model. Of course, what Mekada Graham points out quite explicitly is that these attitudes towards Africans were deeply embedded in the British character. The first English slave ship was named *Jesus* and the first two rules that Captain Hawkins gave to his crew were to serve God daily and to love one another. Obviously Africans were considered to be outside the circle of the religion, the community, or the human race. How can such tremendous ideas of superiority and inferiority be dealt with once they have infected the very social institutions that are supposed to serve an entire multi-cultural community? Mekada Graham has proposed for Britain and, I believe, for the USA, and other multicultural societies, a way to approach social welfare that is based on an appreciation of all cultures.

Social Work and African-centred Worldviews demonstrates the efficacy of an ethnic-sensitive model for intervention in dealing with black family problems in Britain. In this regard Mekada Graham has established what such a model should look like and how it should function. Certainly she has punched a hole in the false conceptions of 'black culture' often paraded in the press and media as indicative of the basic values of blacks in Britain. For Graham, the cultural elements that must be considered and infused into the social work construct in order to assist black families are based on classic African values rooted in the historical realities of African people. These elements are not popular street cultures. It is incorrect to assume that what one sees on the streets or in contemporary movies represent the basic values of African people. Popular street cultures are truly the most representative edge of white materialist culture: for example, the individualistic search for wealth and glitter. This is the antithesis of African cultural values.

A growing body of literature highlights the value of culture in the con-struction of a social work model for heterogeneous, multicultural societies. Such work suggests that Eurocentric ideas have so dominated research and practice that all cultural infusions appear to be either for or against the Eurocentric status quo. Even objections to Eurocentrism are seen as articu-lating European ways of objecting. In other words, all things are collapsed into Europe or else they are not understood. The extent of the domination of the structure of the knowledge as well as the interventions that derive from the knowledge is such that one must first question the authority itself, otherwise the arrogance of a European assumption of its position as the sole determiner of truth continues without question. By not questioning we all remain trapped in a world of illusion, the inclusion illusion. So when Graham writes of the ability of Africans to assess their own cultural values, she is saying that no one has the right to deprive an African of this value. What Graham knows and states is that alternative centres of knowledge are necessary for the advancement of social work. This is true despite the fact that blacks might be practitioners within a Eurocentric system and will undoubtedly continue to have the difficult task of educating their colleagues and indeed, teachers, about the nature of African cultural values. To have black social workers is absolutely necessary but it is not sufficient for a guarantee that children or families will benefit from their efforts. There must be a definite application of new, innovative ethnic-sensitive interventions to make a consistent, regularised difference in success.

Mekada Graham stands at the forefront of a new generation of Afrocentric scholars who have taken the conceptual ideas of the pioneers and launched them into new areas of science. There is a large body of materials developed over the past quarter of a century that addresses issues of identity, culture, values, rehabilitation and social reconstruction. Scholars such as Na'im Akbar, Wade Nobles, Kobi Kambon and Linda James Myers have been leaders in psychological Afrocentricity. Others such as Jerome Schiele, Miriam Maat Ka Re Monges, Nah Dove and Thaddis Mathis have taken the position that social work needs to be reconceptualised. Methodological Afrocentrists, as Ali Mazrui calls them, such as Danjuma Modupe, Kariamu Welsh Asante, Mark Christian, Marimba Ani, Katherine Bankole, Ama Mazama and James Conyers are writing or re-writing chapters in this field. Mekada Graham's book takes the intellectual foundation of Afrocentricity to heart and thrusts it into the centre of the discussion about social work reform, creating new knowledge and giving us new ways of approaching human social welfare. Graham's work underscores the need for alternative social science paradigms that affirm the 'traditions, history and visions' of African people. She states that the principles and values that underpin the African-centred worldview are:

- the interconnectedness of all things
- the spiritual nature of human beings
- collective/individual identity and the collective/inclusive nature of family structure

- oneness of mind, body, and spirit
- the value of interpersonal relationships

This work will remain the classic volume in the reorientation of social work in the current economy of a multicultural heterogeneous Britain. Gifted as a writer, Mekada Graham has articulated the various tensions within the social welfare system in ways that will be understood by social planners, social scientists and social practitioners for years to come. All scholars and organic intellectuals will benefit from the careful, logical, and rational presentation of this work; but surely, the people who will be served by the social workers who understand this perspective will be the greater beneficiaries. In the end, perhaps we shall all lead fuller and happier lives because Mekada Graham has taught us how to respect and honour different values and cultures.

Molefi Kete Asante
Professor, Africology
Temple University, Philadelphia

Acknowledgements

This book is the result of a collective enterprise. I use the term collective in the sense that this work stands on the shoulders of eminent black scholars engaged in the process of reclaiming, recuperating and revitalising cultural knowledge systems of the past in order to assist in building futures and visions for African people throughout the world. Moreover, over the past decades there has been a profusion of literature emanating from black and minoritised scholars highlighting the importance of knowledge systems that continue to inform the cultures, histories, philosophies, traditions, ideas and values of black communities in the diaspora. They have argued that in spite of the influence of assimilationist strategies and the ambiguities in the representations of black people in Britain, black communities maintain strong connections with Africa and the Caribbean.

Scholars such as Molefi Kete Asante, Na'im Akbar, Ali Mazuri, Linda Myers, George Sefa Dei, Ifi Amadiume, Marimba Ani, Jerome Schiele, Marenga Karenga, Wade Nobles and Nah Dove have been a source of inspiration. These inspirational works have provided the impetus for this intellectual work within the context of the struggles and experiences of black communities generally. Their determination and vision to strive and thrive in the face of adverse forces, obstacles and racism is a testament to the human spirit.

One of the defining features of social work is its mission to promote social justice and social change through the empowerment of vulnerable groups in society. These overarching values give rise to an interrogation of forms of oppression not only within the profession and its operations but also within patterns of cultural representation and ideology deeply ingrained within social work knowledge itself. These understandings call into question the staid, narrow and traditional approach to social work that defines a set of boundaries as the sum total of the human experience. Moreover, social work has a commitment to contextual knowing that enables social workers to recognise the diverse vantage points found in one's historical, cultural, spiritual and physical space.

I have worked in the social work profession for almost twenty years and during this period I have rescued myself from the restrictive and oppressive nature of conventional social work to embrace an understanding of worldviews embedded in knowledge systems around the world. This enlightenment was nurtured in the Caribbean at the University of the West

Indies where I was exposed to a wide range of social work literature from India, Africa and China. These works offered the opportunity to explore various worldviews and philosophical traditions as the basis for social work theory and practice.

Upon my return to Britain, a broader and more enriching understanding of social work continued to underscore my work. I refused to be bogged down with the negativity surrounding the profession of social work prevalent within British society. This is because I have experienced and can envision the potential of social work as a force for social change. These understandings have provided the stimulus for writing this book. Social work takes place all over the world, often grounded in helping skills emanating from within the context of local communities. Social work can learn from these skills and talents exercised in pursuit of social wellbeing.

Social workers in black-led organisations have made an important contribution to the struggles and successes of black communities. One of the first black organisations to call upon black social workers was Marcus Garvey's organisation during the early part of the twentieth century (Martin and Martin, 1985). This tradition of seeking the skills and talents of social workers has continued in the new organisations that have emerged in London and elsewhere in recent years. Models of social welfare in various forms within groups and organisations have made an important contribution to black communities. These community activities have highlighted the importance of cultural resource knowledge that encompass physical, intellectual, emotional and spiritual dimensions. These experiences bring to the fore an understanding of empowerment through social relationships and gatherings with others. These gatherings often invite participation from everyone in the group and, through the channel of call and response experiences, the power of the word is strengthened, evoking forms of energy, renewal and spiritual empowerment. This process speaks to lived realities, abiding faith and hope in the possibilities of particular futures and way of life.

I am mindful that I have not discussed in any great detail the work of black churches and other religious organisations in this book. However, I acknowledge their important contribution to social welfare activities, which historically have been linked to black political organisations in pursuit of social justice and a fairer society in Britain.

Special thanks to Dr Nah Dove for her friendship and support. I give thanks and praises to my personal friends, Yvonne, Zophora, Jennifer, Patsy,

Blossom, Makeda, Denise and Eureka. Thank you for your sistering! I also thank Mallum, Bill and Dekenu and others who have allowed me to draw upon their strengths and helped me to identify mine in order to keep on going, and who have encouraged me to write and to keep on writing to complete this book.

My gratitude to Tau Napata and the Ausar Auset Society.

Thank you, Dr Femi Biko, for showing me the way and sharing your wealth of knowledge.

I am grateful to Dr Hakim Ali, Senior Lecturer, Middlesex University for useful comments and suggestions on an early draft of Chapter 3.

My gratitude goes out to Dr Martin Hewitt, Senior Lecturer, University of Hertfordshire, for his strong support, openness and useful criticism of several chapters of this book.

My love and respect for my daughter, Michelle, for without her help and support this book would still be 'in progress', and also to my twins, Safiya and Mekala, and son, Trevor.

Finally, I give thanks and praises to the ancestors who made this work possible.

Portions of Chapter 5 previously appeared in 'The African-centred worldview – developing a paradigm for social work', *British Journal of Social Work*, 29(2) pp. 251–67.

Chapter 1
Introduction

At the beginning of a new century, one of the consistent features of social work education in Britain has been the dearth of social work texts, which consider and address diverse worldviews and social philosophies as a theoretical base for models of social work practice.

Social workers have always dealt with a myriad of tasks, needs and issues that have been shaped and defined by socio-economic, political and cultural contexts. Descriptions of social work, its nature and purpose derive from philosophical presuppositions embedded within Western epistemology, logic and aesthetics. These understandings provide social workers with an appreciation of the historical and philosophical contingencies framing contemporary policy and practice. Thus, in various ways, social work mirrors the social, political and economic concerns, issues and priorities of contemporary society. The purpose of social work, its operations and its practices have been subject to numerous and profound changes over time. The growing importance of social work as an activity, which seeks social change through empowerment in modern society, strengthens the need to examine its knowledge base as the dominant mode of thought in addressing the needs of black communities. (I use the terms 'black' and 'African' interchangeably to refer to all peoples who trace some ancestral or cultural affinity to continental Africa: that is, all those of African descent or who define themselves as black/African.) Over the past decades black activists and practitioners have been critical of social work institutions that sometimes reinforce patterns of discrimination and disadvantage and are often regarded by black communities as yet another 'system' of institutional racism (V. Harris, 1991).

Similarly, there have been concerns about social work interventions with black families that have initiated controversy, conflict and disquiet. These challenges to social work and its operations resulted in attempts to address racism within the profession.

During the 1980s, the Central Council for Social Work Training acknowledged the 'endemic nature of racism in the values, attitudes and structures of British society'. These statements, endorsed by the Central Council for Education and Training in Social Work (CCETSW), were confirmed by the series of events that led to the Stephen Lawrence Inquiry (1999). The subsequent Macpherson Report (1999) substantiated what black people had been

1

voicing for many years: racism permeates the structures and institutions of British society.

This critique is presented against the background of a sustained over-representation of black people across social welfare statistics: for example, black children in the public care system, black people subject to compulsory admissions to psychiatric units, the juvenile justice system and in official school exclusion data (Skellington and Morris, 1992; Barn, 1993; Barn, Sinclair and Ferdinand, 1997; Social Exclusion Unit, 1998). This situation has remained constant for several decades with no obvious strategic plan to arrest these disturbing statistics and turn the tide. The situation facing black communities at the beginning of a new century demands urgent attention.

The primary response to these concerns has been the adaptation of existing models of social work, with special attention being given to racism and cultural differences. Anti-discriminatory practice (which now incorporates anti-racist practice) and the ethnic-sensitive model in the USA have emerged as the most appropriate paradigms than can assist and best meet the needs of black families. For example, Dominelli (1997) and Ahmad (1990) have provided a well-documented exposition of racism in social work and the need to construct anti-racist strategies as part of 'good' social work practice. Existing models of anti-racist social work question power relationships in society in producing and reproducing race and gender sources of oppression. On the other hand, ethnic-sensitive models seek to infuse cultural sensitivities into existing models of social work. Although these models serve a useful purpose in identi-fying sources of oppression located in social work institutions and their operations, they fail to acknowledge sources of oppression that relate to the nature of social work knowledge itself.

Western forms of knowledge currently dominate social work models and approaches. This is because the origins of professional social work can be found in emerging Western industrial societies based on the values of eighteenth-century enlightenment philosophies. Moreover, European/Western academic and professional modes of communication have emerged as powerful conduits in the production of knowledge and its dissemination. This intellectual hegemony lays claim to philosophical and scientific knowledge that is worthy of being called knowledge. This definition of knowledge has tended to evoke power to control the social discourse, subjugating the knowledge and the truths of oppressed people (Hartman, 1994a). It is the power relationships in the legit-imacy of knowledge, its production and dissemination that shape and define its hierarchical nature. This is the domain where the 'other' is associated with 'inferior' forms of knowledge. In this way, power and knowledge are inextricably linked to the process of knowledge production (Foucault, 1977). Therefore, the hegemony of conventional social work knowledge and its dissemination cannot be separated from social, political and economic hegemony within social welfare institutions and the wider society (Schiele, 1997). The question of power relationships gives rise to this hidden source of oppression located within social work knowledge, which continues to remain unchallenged. As O'Brien and Penna (1998a:59) maintain:

> *the whiteness of social services is not simply an issue about numbers of people from different ethnic groups providing or receiving them. It refers to the conventions, assumptions, norms, rules and resources that predominate – culturally and institutionally – and their public whitening of the claims and counterclaims of marginalised groups.*

These assertions draw attention to the centrality of Eurocentric knowledge as the norm and its universal application, which have served to oppress and disempower black families, communities and individuals.

Social work derives its knowledge from theory and research in many different disciplines, all of which have largely been shaped and defined by Enlightenment philosophies. This prevailing approach to knowledge is located in 'expert knowledge', which is inextricably bound to Eurocentric, male social understandings of the world (Martinez-Brawley, 1999). As a consequence, conventional knowledge has been shaped by one-dimensional experiences, values and views of the world which are then seen as standard for all human beings. In this context, social work has often prescribed dominant helping approaches as universally applicable in the concepts and methods set out for all families. Therefore, conventional social work has failed to explore and include forms of knowledge outside Europe as its theoretical base for practice. These considerations call for social work to re-evaluate its approach to knowledge in the light of its underpinning value system that holds human knowledge as infinite: 'each discovery contributes to our knowledge, and each way of knowing deepens our understanding and adds another dimension to our view of the world' (Hartman, 1990:3).

Hartman (1994b) considers social work ideally placed to search for subjugated knowledge because social workers have traditionally served marginalised groups that have long been silenced due to the mechanics of social oppression.

Under these circumstances, human knowledge has no neutral boundaries or objectivity and therefore gives rise to a matter of position/standpoint. It is a matter of where one speaks, to whom and for what purpose that frameworks of knowledge are chosen and adapted for social work theory and practice. Insights such as these provide the context in which minoritised communities and subjugated groups in society often experience 'the world [as] different, untidy, not value-free and objective but value-laden and political' (Martinez-Brawley, 1999:338).

On the margins – exploring subjugated knowledges

The exploration and examination of subjugated knowledge systems draws attention to the continuing historical neglect and marginalisation in the processes of knowledge production, particularly within European/Western contexts. The consequences of marginalisation have resulted in the denial of the space to explore their importance in the social realities and daily lives of black people, families and communities. This exclusion becomes critical given the power imbalance between groups in society in the legitimisation of knowledge and their access to knowledge production and its dissemination (Dei, 1999d).

The marginalisation and suppression of alternative knowledge systems denies the space to interrogate them as a form of resistance and empower-ment. Interestingly, the knowledge claims framing feminist discourse have been interrogated and their space and legitimacy established within academic scholarship. Yet knowledge claims emanating from minoritised groups and their worldviews have received less attention and are often met with scepticism. For example, Bar-On (1999) considers 'non-Western' voices to be largely nothing more than recycled Western ideas. This position is by no means confined to a few academics. It appears that allowing space for other culturally-based epistemology remains somewhat problematic for European social thought in that stepping outside traditional paradigms seems to provoke a measure of discomfort.

Nevertheless, this marginality has created an intellectual space where the understanding of the dynamics of domination and its disruption through the institutionalisation of knowledge provide the impetus for a creative discourse. A creative discourse challenges the complacency of conventional thought to provide a framework of empowerment and dialogue (Dei, 1999d). Therefore, this book necessitates challenge to Eurocentric knowledge as the only valid way of knowing. This assertion is important because of the dominance of Western forms of knowledge in the production and dissemina-tion of social work discourse. Social work is a normative profession organised around a collection of assumptions and frameworks that defines reality as largely fixed and singular. This definition of reality tends to construct a view that only one reality is legitimate and therefore worth speaking about. Yet it is through the production and dissemination and practice of social work knowledge that everyday decisions are made, priorities are defined, in assessments resources are allocated, in varying ways, social problems and their resolutions are shaped and delineated. The cut and thrust of everyday experiences of social workers do not require us to think about the nature of social work knowledge. However, the processes of knowledge production and dissemination are particularly pertinent to this discussion because traditional social work models and approaches have been largely ineffective and sometimes oppressive in addressing the needs of black families and communities.

In a similar way, the lack of appropriate preventative support services and a lack of understanding of the cultural orientation of black families has often resulted in social work operating against the interests of black families and children (Macdonald, 1991; Barn, 1993). Services that are available within existing institutions or professional services are sometimes regarded by black communities as culturally inappropriate or insensitive to their needs.

Under these circumstances, the central force of challenge and resistance posed by alternative knowledge systems centres upon Eurocentric knowledge (that is, Enlightenment thought) masquerading as a universal body of theories and ideas. In this way, Eurocentric knowledge is advanced as the only valid way of knowing. Scheurich and Young (1997:7) draw attention to the ways in which norms 'become so deeply embedded that they typically are seen as "natural" or appropriate norms rather than as historically evolved social constructions'.

The history of ideas emanating from Enlightenment philosophies played a central role in the invention of racial hierarchy through 'codifying and institutionalising both the scientific and popular European perceptions of the human race' (Eze, 1997:5). Thus the history of racism within European social thought has served to subjugate the knowledge systems of people outside Europe. The legitimisation of knowledge became arranged in a hierarchical manner in the same way as racial and gender categories. In this context, subjugated knowledge systems became associated with the 'other' and defined as 'inferior' forms of knowledge. Arising from this process,

power is exercised epistemologically in the dual practices of naming and evaluating. In the naming or refusing to name things in the order of thought, existence is recognised or refused, significance is assigned or ignored, beings elevated or rendered invisible. Once defined, order has to be maintained, serviced, extended, operationalised.
(Goldberg, 2000:155)

These insights provide accounts of forms of history in the constitution of knowledges and discourses which are bound together in the mechanics of a politics of truth and in the relationships of power and knowledge (Foucault, 1972).

Historically, the philosophical foundation of modernity reflected the core assumptions about the nature of human beings, social relationships, cultural value preferences, moral and ethical formulations, and economic, political and welfare considerations. The history of ideas and their philosophical antecedents have informed social work as a source of explanatory theories and therapeutic ideas about human behaviour. The foundations of social work are deeply grounded in philosophical issues. Over time issues such as human need, equality and the role of the state in social welfare have concerned political philosophers and continue to be essential components in contemporary social work.

In this context, Enlightenment philosophies reveal prevailing forms of race and gender exclusion and derogation that hinder the creation of inclusive conditions for equality and social justice. Feminist and black scholars have demonstrated the infusion of racial and gender bias into traditional academic disciplines which are implicated in racist and sexist outcomes (Harding, 1991; Eze, 1997). These philosophical underpinnings have influenced the development of social, political and economic systems over time. Insights such as these have important implications in dissecting core foundations of social work and in understanding its propensity towards hierarchy which is embedded within the quagmire of 'expert' knowledge. Thus, there are historical precedents in knowledge deemed relevant and appropriate for social work which have been largely politically defined and located in the purposes of social work (Howe, 1997). This political definition of legitimate knowledge resides in the notion of universality and dominance expressed within the mechanics of modernity that obviates the multiplicity of knowledge systems of subjugated groups as the basis for social work practice and helping interventions. In other words, social work derives its knowledge from theories, concepts and research based upon the representations of the central philosophical and epistemological commitments of European social thought. Bearing this in mind, conventional studies and theoretical models of race have largely shaped and defined contemporary social work theory and practice with black families.

Thus, conventional social science paradigms of assimilation, cultural deprivation and adaptation underpin models that explain the structure and functioning of black families and communities. The adoption of these approaches has resulted in a social problem paradigm to explain behaviours of black families and communities (English, 1974; Mercer, 1984; Asante, 1990; Dominelli, 1997).

Similarly, the field of psychology with its origins entangled in racist theories has remained firmly entrenched within constructs that serve to dislocate and pathologise black people (Thomas and Sillen, 1972; Mercer, 1984; Robinson, 1995; Dominelli, 1997). It may be argued that it is difficult to find examples of explicit scientific racism in social science theories today. However, Goldberg (2000) provides a useful exposition of 'racial knowledge' located in the social sciences. He argues, for example, that this form of knowledge production is evident in the analysis of the notion of the underclass. Goldberg (2000: 169) suggests this concept is nominated into existence and may under-estimate the disadvantage black people experience, irrespective of their class position. In so doing, 'the notion of the underclass explicitly erases the exclusionary experiences, of racisms from social science analysis while silently enthroning the demeaning impact of race-based insinuations and considerations'. Goldberg (2000:171) argues that conceptual orders such as the underclass are conceived primarily through racialised power located in the social sciences where 'power is . . . expressed, managed and extended in and through representing racial Others– to themselves and to the world'. Subtle forms of scientific racism emerge couched in terms that circumvent racist connotations. This bias has passed into the dominant culture as 'truths' shaping attitudes, institutional practices and policies (Akbar, 1976; Nobles, 1985; Robinson, 1995).

Traditionally, black scholars and researchers have been locked into Eurocentric philosophies and value systems in shaping a frame of reference as the context for analysis of the black experiences and social realities. For many decades black scholars have identified limitations and bias in conventional research methodology. As a consequence of this process, research findings have sometimes produced distorted views of black family life. A new generation of black and minoritised scholars challenged the hegemony of Eurocentric knowledge and demanded a space to examine a multiplicity of worldviews and knowledge systems to establish their legitimacy across the spectrum of human knowledge (Akbar, 1985; Nobles, 1985; Asante, 1987; Schiele, 1994; Scheurich and Young, 1997).

Black communities asserting agency through cultural knowledge and critical consciousness

These aforementioned considerations provide the impetus for urgent rethinking and new directions in social work to develop paradigms and

7

approaches that are effective and appropriate. New directions require innovative strategies, inventions and programmes that not only speak to black communities but stand rooted in their past histories, philosophies and cultures (Dei, 1999d). In this way, cultural resource knowledge can assist in empowering black families and communities to find viable and workable solutions to difficulties experienced by families and individuals.

This is the challenge undertaken by a new generation of black scholars in generating social theory predicated upon an underlying assumption which 'places the African person at the centre of analysis' asserting the African person subject, and not object, of study (Asante, 1990). The African-centred enterprise seeks to organise, study and analyse cultural data in the cultures and philosophies of African people under the umbrella of African-centred social thought. Black scholars reject traditional representations of black peoples immersed in notions of fragmentation, separation, loss and victimisation and instead embrace human agency and empowerment.

Black scholars and researchers have been engaged in developing theoretical and practice models that reflect and affirm the values and worldviews of African people whatever their geographical location (see, for example, Akbar, 1976; Asante, 1988; Everett, *et al.*, 1991; Schiele, 1994). Social workers and scholars from black communities have begun to affirm and integrate their cultural values and worldviews into their scholarship and professional practice (P. Hill, 1992; Schiele, 1997; Graham, 1999).

The affirmation of subjugated knowledges presents challenges of contradictions, questions of representation, ambivalence, misinterpretations and misunderstandings. The notion of tradition and the claim of authenticity have often been the domain of contention and critical debate: for example, the notion of tradition invites possibilities of the invention of a mythical and idealised past. This criticism is often levelled at black scholars in their attempts to reclaim and articulate cultural heritage evident within the social realities and lives of black people and their families, social and political groups and organisations. Questions of tradition and authenticity are related to who has authority in articulating comparative knowledge systems. For example, Western/European scholars have lost authority as subordinate groups redefine and reassess academic scholarship about themselves. Many communities have insisted that they have the right to tell their own stories and histories on their own terms (Tuhiwai Smith, 1999). They have questioned the idea that others know and understand them better than they know and understand themselves.

For many black communities the past reflects the history, custom, cultural practices, ideas and values handed down from generation to generation. This constitutes a past that informs the group's cultural identity. Therefore, the past is not a passive legacy constructed without reference to recent social and political contexts (Dei, 1999d).

This book contributes to the literature of many black and minoritised scholars who write from the standpoint of their philosophies and scientific traditions. This approach offers a 'critique of the wholesale degradation, disparagement and discard of the "traditional" and "culture" in the interest of the so-called "modernity" and the "global space" (Dei, 1999c:11). This domain envelops a space where historical truths, tradition, oratory, metaphysical and material cultures are empowering to black communities living in European societies. The affirmation of these knowledge systems provides the vehicle for affirming their humanity to resist the severing of their past, history and cultures from themselves. It is within this context and framework that black people exercise intellectual agency in engaging in a process of reclamation and revitalisation of knowledge systems, such as African-centred thought, that invites empowerment. As Dei (1999d: 9) maintains, the project therefore 'interrogate[s] the African past, culture, tradition and history in order to learn from its sources of empowerment and disempowerment as African peoples search for ways towards the future'.

Black communities, organisations, families and groups are speaking about knowledge in terms of 'freedom from mental slavery'. This is where group identities become their realities in self-emancipation. This is an integral part of the decolonisation process that has to take place and that draws upon 'the ability to conceptualise the world in ways continuous with one's history' (N. Harris, 1992:158). The affirmation of cultural knowledge can be empowering and assist in social transformation to enable people to break away from dominant ideologies that have shaped and defined their social realities. This space provides the vehicle for cultural re-alignment in 'placing African ideals at the centre of any analysis that involves African culture and behaviour' (Asante, 1987:9). The cultural aspects of Africanity and critical consciousness manifested in the social formations and practices of black families, communities and organisations continues to be a powerful resource base in assisting black people to affirm their spiritual, emotional, and intellectual potential and experiences in the diaspora.

One of the greatest challenges facing black communities and their knowledge systems (such as African-centred worldviews) is the maintenance of the spiritual as well as the material realms of life in the face of continuing marginalisation, exclusion and insidious aspersion. The subjugation of African identities has become more problematic than ever before as the 'modern' denigrates and dismisses the African past and the importance of its legacy in the lives of people of African descent. These challenges do not negate the acknowledgement and recognition of the cultural diversity and shifting identities among African people. On the contrary, the diverse groups and organisations across the broad spectrum of African-descended communities, from black churches to Pan-African movements, vary significantly in the internalisation and demonstration of the cultural ethos of traditional African societies and, moreover, in their acceptance of and pride in Africa as an ancestral homeland. Indeed, African-centred epistemologies cover a broad terrain of realities that must avoid privileging one view over another. This means that there are different ways of being 'black' located in the life worlds and experiences of the diaspora. Nevertheless, cultural resource knowledge can assist in creating opportunities for African people within the diaspora to connect and create a way of being and thinking that is congruent with African values. Within this context, it is all too easy to suppress or ignore the cultural ethos and expressions of Africanity in the social realities of people within the diaspora, particularly when they have been taught to separate themselves from Africa and Africans. Moreover, the historical cultural defamation of Africa and its people has been a defining feature of British society.

Black communities in contemporary society are constant reminders of Britain's imperial and colonial past. Hall (1996:67) suggests that these histories are 'forgotten in the desire to throw off the embarrassing reminders of Empire'. However, for many black communities this historical legacy is a reminder of the impossibility of forgetting the African past and culture. Moreover, the process of dehistorising the contributions of African people and their knowledge systems is part of the colonial and imperialist project (Dei, 1999c).

Communities, groups and organisations provide an important domain where the cultural knowledge resource base affirms and maintains their authority, agency and self-determination. The notion of a black community (or even communities) evokes derision from critiques that assert that we are now all individuals and there is no visible black community. The notion of community can refer to a form of resistance, informed by critical discussion in pursuit of social change. This notion of community speaks to the interdependence of people, their sense of collective history, loyalty and commitment (Dei, 1999d). For example, the Stephen Lawrence Inquiry evoked a sense of community across the spectrum of diverse groups, from the black churches to Pan-African organisations and the Nation of Islam, as the sense of outrage and injustice was experienced in a way that raised a collective consciousness. Within this context, community can operate as an enabler or mobilising force for social justice. This complex reading of community contradicts the assertion that denies the existence of black communities. Dei (1999d: 14) affirms the view that 'while not everyone sees her/himself as belonging to a "community", this "fact" cannot serve as the basis for denying the existence of community'.

Black community groups have traditionally asserted their right to organise and unite around common interests that embraced linkages with other black organisations outside Britain. Many organisations embrace the tenets of Marcus Garvey's philosophy which considers that the only real way to become an integrated and secure being within oneself is to govern and control one's own environment and activities. In this way, black communities continue to manifest an acute understanding of what their interests are, and mobilise to meet them (Phillips, 1982).

Over the past decades African-centred knowledge has gained momentum in black communities in part due to the non-acceptance of African people within British society and the refusal of some people of African descent to be assimilated into British cultural and social formations. African-centred knowledge has been utilised through the popularity of Kwanzaa and the institutionalisation of cultural values within various social welfare activities. These approaches have been largely ignored by social work as sites of empowerment and social change in the pursuit of community regeneration and spiritual renewal.

The author of this book approaches the discourse with a personal, professional and academic interest in articulating the rich cultural heritage emanating from African philosophical knowledge systems that continues to play an important part in the daily lives of people of African origin/descent in Britain today. My early educational experience was one that laid little emphasis on the achievements of African peoples on the continent and throughout the diaspora, or on their knowledge systems, and in particular their contributions to academic scholarship in world civilisations. My education for the most part has not cultivated self-esteem or pride as a person of African descent in the diaspora. All black people of African descent share a common experience of cultural denigration in European/Western contexts as a result of the invention of race and racial hierarchy that led to the enslavement of millions of Africans, dehumanisation, enslavement, colonialisation, struggle, as well as common historical and cultural origins.

As a black scholar I am cognisant of the dangers in academic circles of the very act of writing 'black' which invites risks of misinterpretation, assault and abuse in the pursuit of a critical and oppositional discourse (Dei, 1999d). Holdstock (2000) discusses the antipathy in Western academic circles towards African-centred worldviews. This is expressed in the scant amount of journal space in mainstream journal publications given to Afrocentric scholarship. As L. Myers (1988:4) observes 'the intellectual imperialism of Western patriarchy has proven to be viciously intolerant of any perspective that breaks the bond of its conceptual incarceration' (cited in Holdstock, 2000:112).

In this respect, the considerations discussed in this book lay bare the unspoken rules of power that constantly reshape and redefine the boundaries of conventional discourse and in so doing invite the reactivation of forms of resistance, struggle, creativity and a dogged refusal to be intimidated by existing paradigms. This project necessitates an examination of cultural ideology embedded within the nature of social work knowledge.

The demise of modernity and the emergence of alternative worldviews

In recent years, numerous scholars have challenged the tenets of modernity that lay claim to universal truths based upon the belief in a single reality derived from a single rationality or discourse (Derrida, 1981; Lyotard, 1984; Bauman, 1991). The postmodern discourse dismantles the essential and foundational knowledge that emerged from the Enlightenment era as a central characteristic of modernity. In this way, the postmodern project envelops the claims to knowledge by groups traditionally excluded along the lines of race, gender and class. Thus, the paradigm shift inherent in the demise of modernity enables space for different ways of knowing to join the table of human knowledge.

This paradigm shift ruptures the social constructs of 'the Western man as the norm and measure of humankind' (West, 1989:3) to create a space for a multiplicity of knowledge claims. African-centred knowledge systems have emerged as one of the voices long silenced in the global discourse of Eurocentric intellectual hegemony.

Although recent trends in postmodern thinking have been useful in the challenge and rupture of intellectual hierarchy, this social construct reveals several flaws located in notions of fragmentation and individualisation in shaping human identities. In this way, postmodern theorising as a whole tends to suppress and exclude collective experiences and histories of black people (hooks, 1996). This position denies the importance of black identities as part of a unified experience located in the dynamics of resistance to the structures of power and knowledge (Dei, 1999a).

West (1989) and Young (1990) draw attention to the ethnocentric nature of this standpoint and suggest that postmodern thinking has emerged in response to the decentring of Europe, the decolonising of colonial peoples and the demise of European domination. For West (1989), postmodern theory is essentially a European project characterised by a view of the modern as its frame of reference. This notion of the modern has historically been used to devalue and oppress peoples outside Europe. In this context, it is useful to consider Hill-Collins's (1991:201) viewpoint that all specialised knowledge 'reflect[s] the interests and standpoint of its creators'. In addition, all knowledge systems are sites and sources of possibilities as well as limitations.

Nevertheless, postmodern influences upon the theoretical base of social welfare represent a shift that has opened up intellectual spaces for minoritised and subjugated groups to voice their lived experiences and exert legitimacy in their claims to knowledge.

In the social welfare domain, postmodern constructs have shifted away from universal welfare assumptions and towards an emphasis upon a subjective understanding of welfare recipients as active participants. In a similar vein, questions have arisen about the field of social work and the privileged position of an 'objective' view of reality. The new epistemological paradigms arising from postmodern thinking bring into sharp focus the limitations of conventional social work knowledge and its legitimacy in the light of growing demands for pluralism, not only between groups but also between epistemologies and worldviews. This diversification of knowledge in social work gives voice to the ways in which individuals and communities shape their world through ways of knowing and thinking.

Social work in the twenty-first century
The hallmark of the social work profession has been its emphasis upon promoting humanitarian values. These core principles of social work have their historical foundation firmly grounded in concepts of social justice and a commitment to equality and self-determination as an integral part of its professional ethos (Banks, 1995). Indeed, it has been argued that the profession of social work is unique in this regard because the subject of values and ethics has been central to the development of social work since its formal inception (Wakefield, 1993; Reamer, 1994).

In contrast to other helping professions such as psychology, psychiatry and counselling, social work's long-standing allegiance to a value-based mission embraces a distinctive ethical framework. Thus social work is anchored in concerns about conceptions of fairness, social justice, social exchange, reciprocity and equality. Wakefield (1993) contends that the social justice characteristic of social work serves as the 'altruistic conscience' of society. In many respects these concerns were based upon the 'clients' in early social work where their moral attributes played an important role in social work's mission to ameliorate destitution and poverty. Although the themes of ethics and values have changed considerably in terms of their meanings and emphasis upon social work practice, they remain essential aspects of the foundation of social work knowledge.

Bearing these considerations in mind, it is necessary to examine the various dynamics, meanings and understandings of social work values and ethics in order to assist in promoting the realisation of social work's goals and mission towards social change. The inclusion of a multiplicity of worldviews, including African-centred ways of knowing, can initiate conceptual frameworks for new social work practice models. Thus, the key social work tasks that require the integration of the values and ethics of the profession can satisfy human needs by embracing a new vision of possibility. One of the primary social work ethics and values relates to the infinite possibilities of human knowledge created in the ongoing search for models of excellence in human life. This legitimate and constructive debate about the nature and boundaries of social work knowledge constitutes important intellectual work in defining and redefining the profession's theoretical base. Discourse and debate about forms of knowledge are critical to the growth and development of the profession.

Bar-On (1994:53) draws attention to the boundaries of the professional concern as defined in the here and now that reflect needs not being met by society's primary institutions. In this way, social work has been defined as a 'residual institution with boundaryless areas of concern'. These concerns about the boundaries of social work are tethered to its knowledge base and add further complications in articulating a foundation for social work. The breadth and diversity of this domain provides the site where conventional ideas are questioned in the light of social changes and conditions. These considerations serve as the rationale for the expansion of existing boundaries of legitimate knowledge to satisfy human need. In line with this thinking, African-centred paradigms resonate with core social work principles in promoting humanitarian values in the best of African-centred social thought and practice in dialogue and social exchange with the world.

African-centred social thought considers cultural location, coupled with local knowledge and experience, to be the fundamental source of people's identity, purpose and direction (Karenga, 2000). It is therefore the collective thread of consciousness that creates the logic of liberation in resisting dominant ideologies which have shaped and defined the human condition. Experience and social realities inform this understanding. These are important considerations because the profession of social work rests upon normative ethical and value systems that are grounded in ethnocentric commitments and understandings of the world.

Kuhn (1970) identifies the constituents of unquestioned models of human behaviour that shape and defines social work practice:

paradigms are deeply embedded in the socialisation of adherents and practitioners, telling them what is important, what is legitimate, what is reasonable. Paradigms are normative; they tell the practitioner what to do without the necessity of long epistemological considerations. But it is this aspect of a paradigm that constitutes both its strength and weakness – its strength in that it makes action possible, its weakness in that the very reason for action is hidden in the unquestioned assumptions of the paradigm. (abridged from Kuhn (1970), quoted in Humphries (1995:7)

It is within this context that black communities, organisations, groups and families are speaking about cultural knowledge as an important frame of reference in directing and sustaining community regeneration, renewal and spiritual rebirth. For black communities this involves reclamation, recovery, creating and recreating the best of African culture, which includes the lived experiences of people of African descent in the diaspora. This critical consciousness has been the prerequisite of a long line of black scholars and activists engaged in reconstructing the central features of African-centred worldviews including its philosophical and ethical assumptions, historical and cultural patterns (Diop, 1978; Williams, 1987; Asante, 1988; Asante and Abarry, 1995). These key elements represent not only a concept which categorises a quality of thought but which also represents and reflects the life experiences, history and traditions of African people as the centre of analysis. This approach has resulted in reclamation of the ancient knowledge systems of the classical African civilisations of Kemet, Nubia, Kush and Axum as the baseline for conceptions of human beings and the universe. This project provides scholars with an anchorage in the reconstitution of cultural patterns and philosophies for the benefit of black communities and humanity.

Numerous research studies have shown the retention of cultural 'Africanisms' in the social realities of black families throughout the diaspora (Herskovits, 1958; DuBois, 1969; Alleyne, 1971; Holloway, 1990). These findings are powerful enough to justify a serious interrogation of any attempts to minimise the cultural affinities and ties with continental Africans and African cultures. This approach challenges the long-standing assertions that people of African descent have retained nothing of significance from African culture as the experience of enslavement destroyed all vestiges of and links with, their philosophies and culture. The term 'negro' was imposed and used to describe African people in the New World, together with consistent themes of intellectual inferiority and fragmentation and separation characterising their social domain. These configurations became embedded within theoretical paradigms of cultural deprivation of a group whose culture has developed only as an adaptation to enslavement and poverty.

African-centred social work models assist in shifting focus away from dysfunction and treatment towards social transformation in assisting families in finding solutions to problems in everyday life. Themes of disparagement of Africa and its people have been a consistent feature of British society and in part provide the context in which black communities seek to maintain cultural and spiritual connections, authority and agency through knowledge systems in their everyday social realities. This knowledge affirms black communities as the subjects of their own experiences and histories, and shift the emphasis away from 'victimisation to encompass knowledge for collective resuscitation, spiritual rebirth and cultural renewal' (Dei, 1999d:23)

Cultural resource knowledge can be empowering to black communities and this is where new approaches to social work practice are exercised in response to social need. This approach recognises more than just the importance of cultural background but also seeks to ascertain the various ways in which a critical reading of cultural resource knowledge can be utilised as a means of empowerment. The contribution of African-centred worldviews to social work discourse can be characterised in four ways.

First, the exposition of this culturally based resource can provide useful insights into the hidden sources of oppression within social work knowledge itself. In this way, African-centred approaches to social work can be created to assist in bringing about equality, social justice and social change in a meaningful way.

Second, African-centred social work challenges and ruptures the complacency of conventional social work knowledge. Critical theories such as

African-centred approaches propose a multilevel strategy in which the patterns of conventional knowledge production are scrutinised. An interrogation of social work knowledge counters the misconception that Western social thought holds exclusive rights to knowledge and opens up an intellectual space in which the flurry of black academic scholarship can be affirmed. In so doing, African-centred social work provides a vehicle for power sharing in a real sense as its knowledge base is grounded in philosophies outside Europe that enrich the development of social work knowledge.

Third, African-centred social work can serve to promote models of service delivery, which assist and strengthen community building. This approach requires the recognition and validation of skills and capacities that are often ignored or unnoticed by conventional social work.

Fourth, cultural resource knowledge can create an environment where time-honoured institutions that have sustained communities over time are utilised in constructing viable and workable solutions to difficulties in families and communities. To practise from a community-building perspective enjoins social workers to be open and attuned to the talents and skills within black communities and to engage in activities that generate strengths, knowledge and competence. This approach is in line with contemporary trends towards a strategic social inclusion agenda, which promotes the importance of embracing communities' own potential for development and regeneration. Insights such as these must necessarily start with subjective accounts of the realities and experiences of the structures and institutional arrangements that affect people's lives in the delivery of social services and health care (John, 1999).

This book is written at a time when there have been increasing demands for social work services to be more accountable and demonstrate effectiveness. The efficacy of conventional social work practice models in working with black families continues to be questioned in the light of challenges to the profession to break down the stranglehold of institutional racism and discrimination.

The history of activism in social work provides a vehicle through which progressive approaches, including African-centred social work, can assist in meeting the challenge to create and sustain a just society and a better world. These possibilities, visions and hopes call for the re-evaluation of social work's mission in consideration of pluralism, not only between groups but also between epistemologies and worldviews. Moreover, the realisation of these possibilities confirms the profession's meaningful participation in social justice and social change.

One of the major challenges facing social work in the twenty-first century centres upon the ways in which the profession responds to cultural diversity. These challenges give rise to demands for a universal pluralistic view of society that acknowledges the multiplicity of world cultures and their contribution to the betterment of humanity. Can the profession translate its humanitarian values of equality into embracing equally valid worldviews that share diverse human realities and experiences, and use these as the basis for social work theory and practice on equal terms?

This book attempts to address this challenge to enable social workers to have a greater appreciation of the theoretical perspectives that can enliven and enrich social work. Ultimately, the aim and purpose of social work is to transform knowledge into meaningful practice. The linking of theory and practice in a purposeful way serves as the cornerstone of our understanding and approach to practice. A central feature of African-centred ways of knowing has been its emphasis upon the connections between theory and practice as a holistic approach to systematic knowledge and social action.

Karenga (1993:19) articulates this stance further in calling for academia to be directed towards service to the community in a 'positive developmental way in the interest of human history and advancement'.

This approach is in line with the growing demands for social workers to incorporate research into their practice and concerns about the quality of services, process and outcomes. So far social work has failed to respond to the opportunities presented in exploring the diverse worldviews and cultures as frameworks of practice. The twenty-first century presents new opportunities in response to social changes which will require social work to broaden and shift its boundaries. These conditions will provide opportunities for social workers to be at the forefront of identifying new arenas of practice.

This book makes an important contribution to the growth and development of social work in articulating cultural resource knowledge as a source of empowerment, social transformation and social change.

Outline of the book

This book seeks to promote cultural resource knowledge as an important source of empowerment for social work in black communities. This introductory chapter has covered a broad terrain whilst identifying the power relationships embedded within Western forms of knowledge. As a result of this process other forms of knowledge, such as African-centred worldviews, have been largely ignored or marginalised in Western/European contexts as the basis for social work theory and practice. This general overview of social work is juxtaposed with its value-based mission which gives rise to important questions concerning the fulfilment of its humanitarian goals of social justice and equality, and social work's role in promoting social change. This section concludes with a challenge to social work to expand its conceptual framework to include a multiplicity of worldviews as legitimate and valid thereby embracing a truly multicultural, theoretical and practice-based profession.

Chapter 2 presents a critical account of Enlightenment philosophies and the ways in which they have shaped and defined contemporary paradigms in social work. These historical contingencies produced conditions of exclusion and the hierarchical bonds of race, gender and class. Moreover, I discuss the legacy of modernity in social constructions of black families that inform social work policies and practice.

Chapter 3 examines the connections between the institution of enslavement and the development of social welfare. I contend that the prevailing attitudes and social beliefs which endorsed the institution of enslavement produced paradigms of extreme human degradation which philanthropists and social reformers drew upon in their efforts to ameliorate the deprivations of the English poor. The institution of enslavement became the baseline or social marker for hierarchical models of poverty and destitution in the treatment and welfare of the English poor. The consequences of enslavement permeated the contours of social welfare, policy and practice during a critical period in the development of the modern welfare state when the free flow of ideas shaped the conceptualisation of welfare instruments (Hendrick, 1994). Moreover, this chapter explores social welfare among a group of people endeavouring to improve their lives but starting from a baseline of enslavement and servitude.

Chapter 4 presents an outline of the central features of African-centred worldviews, including African-centred philosophical assumptions, historical and cultural patterns providing a broad base of information and discussion translated into African-centred perspectives in social work. This intellectual endeavour emerges out of a codification of traditional African, especially West African cultural values, narratives and experieinces into a systematic interpretative framework to explain and resolve social problems. These values, narratives and experiences are not deemed monolithic but are sufficiently distinctive to constitute recognisable cultural patterns over time (Schiele, 2000). I take the view that African-centred worldviews are framed by diversity that shares a common disporean experience of oppression.

19

This chapter explores the central principle of Maat which provides a moral and ethical guide within African-centred worldviews. The central thrust of Maat produces a communal foundation of African culture that highlights the importance of justice and harmony between humans (living, departed and yet to be born) and their material and spiritual worlds. Maat forms the basis of social welfare considerations and a contextual framework for ethical theory building in social work. In this context, this section considers the ethical system of Maat translated into modern moral discourse as a source of theory building for social work. Spirituality is the organising principle of Maat, and within this context the spiritual dimensions of social work are considered.

This chapter also discusses the problematics and critiques of African-centred worldviews that have evoked intense debates among academic circles. This groundwork is expected to heighten recognition of the intrinsic worth of cultural resource knowledge to professionals engaged in theory, practice and research in social work.

Chapter 5 examines the primary response of social work in addressing the needs of black people. The ethnic-sensitive model and anti-discriminatory practice have emerged as the most appropriate paradigms to assist and best meet their needs. Although these models include important areas that must be addressed, limited attention has been given to social work designs that reflect the worldviews and cultural values of diverse communities in Britain. This section reviews the ethnic-sensitive and anti-discriminatory models of social work and provides a critical account of their intrinsic limitations and flaws. This chapter also charts the strengths of black families and examines the empowerment thesis of Solomon (1976) to explore its purposeful resonance with African-centred approaches to social work. Moreover, it considers the importance of cultural resource knowledge in shaping the contours of social welfare in black communities.

Chapter 6 continues to explore social welfare interventions in black-led community organisations as a means and source of empowerment. These sites of intervention reject deficit approaches that tend to characterise conventional social work approaches to embrace culturally affirming models located in cultural knowledge and lived experiences.

This section also charts black-led efforts to spearhead changes in social work policy and practice. The author argues calls for the active involvement of social work in serving the needs of local communities and in creating opportunities and partnerships to develop new approaches to bring about social justice and social change.

Chapter 2
Exploring contours of knowledge in social welfare and social work

The philosophical foundations of social work are seldom discussed in social work literature as the source of understanding human behaviour and patterns of living. Social workers are often so immersed in demands, and sometimes a daunting array of problems and crises, that they have no time or energy to explore the important philosophical underpinnings of their practice. Yet social workers cannot ignore the fact that their practice often reflects philosophical and cultural assumptions about ways of knowing. These ways of knowing involve ethical dimensions of philosophy that provide models of decision making mirrored in the professional behaviours of social workers.

Social work derives its core knowledge from the social sciences, primarily sociology and psychology. These theories of human behaviour, institutions, social, political and economic formations and practices provide the contextual background for the development of social work models of practice. Although social workers also depend upon acquired skills, theoretical knowledge anchors and structures these relationships in a conceptual frame which is orientated towards social action. Theories provide the framework of interconnected concepts that give meaning and explanation to problem-solving efforts and support new insights (Lipsey, 1993). Hartman (1994a:459) further sees that:

> *nothing is more crucial in shaping and defining the social work profession and its practice than that profession's definition of 'the truth' and the selection of preferred strategies for knowledge building. Further, the process through which truth is defined and the methods of truth seeking chosen is highly political.*

In this chapter, I explore the philosophical underpinnings of knowledge that inform theories and therapeutic ideas in models of practice in social work. This critical analysis provides insights into the ways in which social work's philosophical foundations are implicated in creating conditions of exclusion.

The constituents of recognised 'knowledge' in social work

The political nature of 'recognised' knowledge for social work is particularly relevant in Britain because social work operates in the main within state institutions. Thus, as cited by Howe (1997:175) 'in the broadest sense, the purposes of social work are determined by the prevailing political values, so that state institutions determine the purpose, depth and scope of social work leaving little or

21

no room for alternative theory and practice'. Social work, then, has traditionally selected knowledge deemed appropriate and certain preferred instruments for knowledge building in order to shape definitions of the profession's 'truth'. These sources of knowledge support and build upon social processes involved in maintaining control of knowledge and its dissemination.

This body of knowledge deemed relevant and appropriate in conventional social work has its origin in European Enlightenment philosophies. The Enlightenment represents an important epoch in European intellectual history in establishing a form of philosophical thought, which provided the foundations for modern social sciences. The Enlightenment thinkers challenged the existing worldview dominated by religious dogma, superstition and orthodoxy. These conceptions propagated the view that the nature of human beings, the social world and the environment are regulated by the word of God and the divine order. The Enlightenment thinkers were in engaged in a critical examination of all aspects of the social and natural world of human beings. Their analysis of the existing worldview not only focused upon tearing down the old order but building a new framework of knowledge about human beings, nature and the universe. This form of philosophy was no longer a mere abstraction but included the organisation of society and daily life. As Cassirer (1951:viii) concurs, 'Enlightenment thought is not merely reflective, nor is it satisfied to deal solely with axiomatic truths. It attributes to thought a creative and critical function, the power and task of shaping life itself'.

The era of Enlightenment spans the seventeenth and eighteenth centuries with the primacy of reason and rationality characterising the former and the synthesis of the philosophy of rationalism and empiricism to produce a unified methodological model for science and codification of knowledge.

Enlightenment thinkers produced an array of philosophical systems that gave meaning to the relationships between theoretical frameworks and patterns of social welfare. These theoretical ideas gave rise to forms of liberalism, Marxism, structuralism and other economic and political considerations. Moreover, these social and political theories each expressed elements of a theory of knowledge that has its grounding within Enlightenment thought. In addition, it is difficult to understand and appreciate the development of social sciences without an appreciation of the Enlightenment's contribution to their formation and organisation (O'Brien and Penna, 1998b). Debates about the nature of social work and theories of knowledge coupled with the political, social and economic structures of society, developed from philosophical traditions inherited from the eighteenth century. These debates were derived from and expressed social commitments of Enlightenment principles and assumptions such as progress, justice, social reform and reason. Theories of social welfare and social work became tethered to the principles and beliefs of the Enlightenment.

The development of liberal ideology has produced social and political thought that has made important contributions to contemporary social welfare theories, and social and political action. There is not a unified single liberal ideology that encompasses liberal theory. Liberal thinkers differ in their view of the role and functions of individuals, their freedoms and the management of social, political and economic institutions. However, classical liberalism and its links with modernity provided the key elements in shaping social welfare and the management of the poor and destitute. The foundations of liberal philosophy emphasised freedom and autonomy, social progress and the universal spread of reason and the potential of individual human beings. Individualism is the cornerstone of liberal ideology, inviting all state action to have as its goal the maximisation of an individual's pursuit of self-interest. The natural rights of individuals not to be subject to the will of others became a central tenet of liberal philosophy. The guarantee of freedom according to abstract laws, together with moral and economic individualism, formed the building blocks of a liberal approach to the Enlightenment.

The rights of individuals and the protection of those rights in an organised civil society were often the subject of political and social debate. The central theme of the debate focused upon the need for rules and codes of conduct because individuals act in their own interests without necessarily any regard to consequences. The development of a rational society relied upon the premise of rules and codes of conduct to counterpoise individuals acting in their own interests without regard for the consequences for others. They would be 'free' to do as they please. These important questions gave rise to abstract moral and ethical discourses concerning the nature of governance and the moral basis of government.

The nature and extent of state intervention in the lives of individuals has been a long-standing discursive discourse in social policy. The history of social welfare is concerned with the changing balance between individual self-reliance and community responsibility. Liberal philosophy had a vision of progress towards a wealth-producing social order. However, widespread poverty among the poor provided the impetus for an expression of a sense of universal justice that heralded a move towards state welfare. The introduction of Poor Law legislation marked the beginning of state intervention to provide a minimal service for the destitute. Community concern for the plight of the poor and destitute grew as the level of philanthropic activity increased in the late nineteenth century (Heasman, 1962).

The rise of organised charity resonated with the liberal doctrines of self-reliance and individual effort. The prevailing belief that a system of state intervention necessarily undermined individual responsibility and encouraged idleness characterised the philanthropic movement. Philanthropic activity was thought to be at less risk of encouraging idleness and dependency in that charitable aid was not a right but dependent upon genuine need. As charitable works proliferated during the nineteenth century, charity was distributed indiscriminately and no checks were made, concern began to mount about the fraudulent use of charity. This rise in organised charity resulted in more people receiving charity than poor relief. The growing concerns about the misuse of funds provided the impetus for a rational, ordered scientific approach to philanthropy to replace disarray as the best hope of understanding poverty and pauperism.

The Charity Organisation Society (COS) was formed in 1869 to co-ordinate the operation of the Poor Law and the provision of individualised charity. The COS enshrined liberal views of self-reliance and self-help and resisted well into the twentieth century 'every important legislative measure of social welfare' (Fido, 1977:207). The vision of the COS was derived from Enlightenment philosophies as a secular approach to charity whilst producing a 'professional approach' to social work. This shift towards scientific charity marked the beginning of 'helping that was conscientiously rational, in the sense of deliberately relating the means and ends of helping' (Leiby, 1997:360).

The COS devised a scientific approach to philanthropy and conferred the need for factual information to be confirmed within the framework of casework. The COS made possible the rational application of social scientific knowledge to the solution of social problems. The secularisation of charity advanced Enlightenment philosophies which emphasised effective individual and social change through the application of methods derived from scientific rationalism. In effect, science had replaced mystical forces as the principal agent of personal change (Bowpitt, 1998).

There have been numerous accounts of the functions and nature of the COS (Mowat, 1961;Woodroofe, 1962; Rooff, 1972) and its importance to the origins of social work. Marxist writers have provided an interpretation of the social control functions applied by the COS in reasserting class dominance over the working class and resisting collective forms of social welfare (Perkin, 1969; Fido, 1977). Bowpitt draws attention to the 'waging of an ideological and institutional struggle with the churches for the control of philanthropy' (1998:685). The vision of the COS became an early attempt to inject social scientific realism into the understanding of human problems beyond the superficial presentation of need. The 'caseworker', the predecessor of the social worker, applied rational means of investigation to establish professional expertise. This expertise was grounded in a body of knowledge that was seen as 'scientific', thus establishing a scientific base to the new profession of social work. The importance of Enlightenment philosophies is located in the reinterpretation of social improvement away from individual spiritual regeneration and towards science as the path to social transformation. Many COS practitioners believed that scientific philanthropy was the best way of understanding destitution and poverty.

The administration of social assistance aided the development of a 'professional' culture for social work. The COS became an organisation where the exchange of ideas, attitudes and methods derived from Enlightenment ideology of social progress contributed to the development of social work as a profession and a distinct body of knowledge. The society was instrumental in establishing the first School of Sociology in 1903, where social work knowledge became the vehicle for the application of scientifically based principles in a new progressive social movement. The primacy of scientific rationality in understanding and solving destitution and poverty was revealed in the first textbook for social workers.

Mary Richmond (1917), in her work, *Social Diagnosis* proposed that science held precedence in the construction of helping interventions. This scientific approach emphasised a clear, critical and logical approach to thought. She advocated the use of scientific methods to develop the knowledge base of the profession. These early attempts to bring the benefits of scientific methods to bear upon social problems of the era started a long-standing debate about the value and role of science in social work research. These concerns have taken on a similar allegiance in the social sciences as a whole. Searching questions about the best theory of knowledge for social work have fuelled intense debates among social work researchers. At one end of the spectrum, traditional approaches located in quantitative and positivist methods are deemed most effective and 'scientific' in measuring outcomes. On the other hand, researchers such as Heineman (1981) have drawn attention to traditional methods as being antiquated and restrictive; such methods have long been abandoned by primary disciplines in the social sciences. She argues that, as a result of this approach, important questions and valuable information are left unresearched.

A generation of new researchers has questioned the unrelenting preoccupation of social work research with number crunching data to develop models of research that consider and capture the meanings and understandings of individuals and communities. In this way, the complexities and issues from the perspectives of client populations can be researched to provide useful insights into problem solving and designs for social work practice. These changes can be seen to represent a shift away from nineteenth-century charity, which was social control of the poor, to a sophisticated twentieth-century social welfare, which is concerned with social justice, rights and regulation of the poor and disadvantaged.

Enlightenment and the invention of racial hierarchy

This brief overview of contemporary epistemological debates gives an indication of the influence of the Enlightenment and a vision of scientific progress in the field of social welfare in shaping social work as a profession. However, it is sensible at this juncture to consider the central role of Enlightenment philosophies in the invention of racial hierarchy through 'codifying and institutionalising both the scientific and popular European perceptions of the human race' (Eze, 1997:5). The Enlightenment discourse on race has been largely ignored in modern philosophical thought Eze, 1997). Goldberg (1993:7) blames this omission on modernity's liberal traditions and commitments to idealised principles of liberty and equality. These moral imperatives mask its 'racialised history and the attendant histories of racist exclusions, hiding them behind some idealised, self-promoting, yet practically ineffectual, dismissal of race as a morally irrelevant category'. Herein lies the paradox of contemporary liberalism where all is race but race is irrelevant both at the same time (Dei, 1999d). However, the notion of racial hierarchy in social development has been a major theme of modern philosophy.

These considerations are pertinent to social work because the history of ideas and their philosophical antecedents have informed social work as a source of explanatory theories and therapeutic ideas. It is within the foundation of social work knowledge that these principles, ideas and values have shaped social work approaches to social problems and social needs. These approaches are reflected in the range of insights and understanding over time.

Over the past decades, numerous scholars have cogently demonstrated the ways in which racial and sexual hierarchy was developed, refined and disseminated in forms of knowledge that informed and defined social, political and economic formations and institutions (Harding and Hintikka, 1983; Asante, 1987; Goldberg, 1993; Lennon and Whitford, 1994; Scheurich and Young, 1997). These conditions set the context in which 'the Eurocentric focus of social work theory and practice obscures the historical and contemporary consequences of colonialism, the legacy of slavery and the relations of subordination and domination that underpin the white encounter with "other" races' (O'Brien and Penna, 1998:60). It is within the arena of philosophy that core assumptions about the nature of human beings, social relationships, cultural value preferences, moral and ethical foundations are cultivated and are embedded within the foundations of social welfare.

Enlightenment philosophies did not create conditions for equity and social justice. On the contrary, this historical period was marked by enslavement of and violence towards African people, and European imperial incursions into Africa and elsewhere. These complex sets of ideas, beliefs and commitments constructed a hierarchical ranking within philosophical domains that was transferred into social contexts as a unitary stream of thought that envisaged those outside this parameter as 'Other'. This socially constructed self-image 'quickly became those – and only those – who could know fully' (Outlaw, 1996:56).

The dominant tradition in Western philosophy has placed a very high value upon reason and rationality which are characterised in ways that are inextricably tied to European male social understandings of the world. Hegel, Kant, Hume and Descartes sought to articulate a neutral and universally binding framework for rationality that has shaped the core principles of conventional philosophy.

Novak (1972:775) calls for the revision of the notion of reason articulated by philosophers of the Enlightenment:

No one would deny that there is a perfectly straightforward sense in which all human beings are members of the same human family; every human being is bound by imperatives of reasoning, justification, and communication across cultural and other boundaries; and each human being is entitled to claims of fundamental human dignity. Still, it is also

widely grasped today that reason itself operates in pluralistic modes.
It would be regarded as 'cultural imperialism' to suggest only one form
of reasoning is valid in all matters. It would be regarded as naïve to
believe that the content of human experiencing, imaging, understanding,
judging, and deciding were everywhere the same. (quoted in Outlaw,
1996)

Although critics maintain that Western philosophy is too diverse to permit generalisations such as these to be made, there is no doubt that aspects of these legacies have been the driving force in articulating European superiority while simultaneously denigrating Africa, its peoples and knowledge systems. Feminist scholars have explored the male gender patterns that have characterised Enlightenment philosophies, and have alluded to the deep and varied ways in which the ideals and institutions of culture of traditional philosophy oppress women (Lloyd, 1984; Garry and Pearsall, 1992). Feminist scholars argue that conceptions of knowledge and truth widely accepted by society have been shaped and defined throughout history by a male-dominated culture. Men have mostly constructed the main theories, written history and formulated the values that permeate society. As a result of this process, women's contribution to Western social theory has been devalued and marginalised. Some feminist writers contend that there is a masculine bias embedded within most academic disciplines and methodologies and theories (Bernard, 1973; Harding and Hintikka, 1983; Keller, 1985; Belenky *et al.* 1986).

The feminist critique of traditional philosophy interrogates the limitations and bias of particular traditions and fields of philosophy. Under these circumstances, feminist philosophers can identify and detail the ways in which traditional philosophy has undermined women's voices and excluded their life experiences within the key concepts of the discipline. Feminist philosophers have sought to redefine the methods and subject matter of philosophy to enable women to move from a position of object to positions of subject and agency. In this regard, two trends have emerged in philosophical discussions: first, the task of feminising conventional philosophy and second, creating a feminist philosophy in its own right, with its own canon, set of theories and agendas for discussion.

Boneparth (1978) argues in favour of this two-pronged approach in which feminists seek to infuse feminist perspectives into traditional disciplines whilst simultaneously maintaining their independence. For example, feminist scholars claim that women and men are fundamentally different and therefore it is not possible to have a successful merging of scholarship to create a discipline applicable to both men and women. However, there is no doubt that feminist scholarship has assisted in shifting the one-dimensional view of the world in academic contexts to include feminine knowledge. Some feminists have advocated that 'the rules of academy be changed in order to correct the omissions, distortions and trivialisations of women and women's lives (Makosky and Paludi, 1990:15). For example, Bristow and Esper (1988:72) proposed a woman-centred approach to research with the introduction of feminist methodology providing a framework for consciousness raising. In this way, a feminist-based approach in psychological and sociological research ensures 'the reality of women's lives as women themselves define their experience'. In so doing, research 'attempts to bring forth that reality in a manner which frees women's voices from the dominant context which derives power from women's silence'.

In a similar vein, black scholars are engaged in uncovering philosophical writings on 'race' to examine the ways in which Kant and other Enlightenment thinkers contributed to the academic and intellectual codification of racism in European societies as well as exploring links between anthropology and philosophy (Eze, 1999).

Over the past decades philosophers have articulated traditional and contemporary African social thought in both oral and written literatures as forms of philosophy that have brought into sharp focus the absence of persons of African and African descent in mainstream philosophical literature. This body of literature has focused upon the need to include the philosophising of African people in conventional philosophy. However, the primary area of intense intellectual debates has focused upon the validity, legitimacy and academic status of African philosophy. Debates surrounding the place of African philosophy bring to the fore the emergence of African-centred worldviews as an important cultural foundation source in the study of black people, their lived experiences, social practices, survival, wellbeing and understanding of the world (Akbar, 1985; Nobles, 1985; Asante, 1987; Schiele, 1994).

Creating the conditions of exclusion

For Hume, Kant and Hegel, arguably the most influential Enlightenment thinkers of modern times, race was an important subject. The writings on race by Hume, Kant and Hegel articulated European cultural and racial supremacy as a way of explaining difference. Eze (1997) argues that the Enlightenment constitutes the historical period when thinkers were provided with the philosophical and scientific vocabulary of race. Davidson's (1991) work indicates that the earliest recorded encounters of Europe with Africa reveal a relationship between equals. A shift towards the human trade with Africa coincides with the Enlightenment era, which produced a marked philosophical characterisation of African people based upon physical differences.

The ideological conception of race entered the academic, political and social world producing a distinctive hierarchical view of humanity and associated human qualities (Stocking, 1982; Fryer, 1984; Bernal, 1987). Enlightenment thinkers sought to map out the geographical landscape of humanity, its history, and philosophical and moral domains. The Enlightenment produced a powerful striving for classification; fragmentation and binary opposites derived from achievements gleaned from the study of nature. These elements provided the platform for the classification and scientific study of humanity across the globe.

The development of the scientific domains of biology and anthropology provided the focal point for intense activity in the study of human beings outside Europe. Anthropology became 'the science of peoples without history' (Goldberg, 1993:29). Europeans searched for ways to differentiate themselves from 'others'. Within the science of humanity emerged theories of degeneracy. These theories sought to explain why African and indigenous peoples were 'different' from Europeans and attributed to them inferior qualities that rendered them sub-human. It is within the nature of classification that the 'other' is conceived. Thereby as Europeans racialised those denigrated as 'non-white' and the 'other', they simultaneously racialised themselves as white and male and these characteristics became a powerful marker for exclusion and white male privilege (Goldberg, 1993).

People outside Europe were increasingly viewed as inferior and savage. Eze (1997:4) asks the question, 'Why had the concept of race gained so much currency in European enlightenment scientific and socio-political discourse?' The Enlightenment discourse on race played a strong role in articulating Europe's sense of cultural as well as racial superiority. Reason and civilisation was attributed to Europeans, and savagery, primitivism and irrationality became synonymous with 'non-Europeans', black, red and yellow (Eze, 1997). This provided the framework for the legitimacy of European epistemologies whereas the 'other', (African, Asian and indigenous) knowledge systems could never be scientific. Science became synonymous with 'whiteness'.

Hume, Kant and Hegel's writings on race provide useful insights into the invention of a racialised discourse that provided a frame for self-definition as 'mature' human beings capable of reason and rational thought. Thus, those outside this frame were depicted as different, sub-human and incapable of rational thought, lacking in essential human qualities. Hume regarded the understanding of human nature as the key to the secure foundation of all sciences. He wrote: 'the science of man . . . is the only solid foundation for the other sciences and human nature is the only science of man'. (Hume, 1968:37 and 273 quoted in S. Hall and Gieben, 1992:37). Hume's focus upon human nature filters through to the concept of race.

According to Hume (1748), the Africans are naturally inferior to Europeans:

I am apt to suspect the negroes and in general all other species of men (for there are four or five different kinds) to be naturally inferior to the whites. There never was a civilised nation of any other complexion than white, nor even any individual eminent either in action or speculation. No ingenious manufacturers amongst them, no arts, no sciences. On the other hand, the most rude and barbarous of the whites, such as the ancient Germans, the present Tartars, have still something eminent about them. . . . Such a uniform and constant difference could not happen . . . if nature had not made original distinction betwixt these breeds of men. (quoted in Eze, 1997:33)

Hume proposes that there are inherent racial differences delineated by skin colour that are permanent and fixed by nature. Hume's justification for this proposal is grounded in empirical evidence since, according to Hume, no Africans had produced science, art or 'any symptoms of ingenuity'. Empiricism encouraged the tabulation of perceivable differences between people and led to conclusions regarding their natural difference. Hume's propositions placed Africans outside the realms of humanity. These philosophical formulations and the denial of humanity to Africans and groups originating outside Europe were circulated and recycled by European thinkers and reached the *Encyclopedie*. The *Encyclopedie* was an important and influential work that covered virtually all of the major philosophies and viewed the reduction of science into one document as the supreme form of knowledge.

The circulation of these beliefs was apparent in Kant's many essays on race that ascribed evidence of rational thought and human capacity on the basis of skin colour. Kant's (1775) statement that 'this man was black from head to toe, a

31

clear proof that what he said was stupid' appealed to Hume's propositions on race mentioned earlier. Kant endorsed Hume's correlation between nature and race and turned racial subordination into an *a priori* principle.

The enslavement of Africans was predicated upon their alleged 'sub-humanity'. Hegel's thesis on Africa and Africans proposed that the movement of human history corresponded to the emancipation of human consciousness. According to Hegel, history is understood as a sequence of stages. Human consciousness is manifested in social and political institutions. History is the trail of human consciousness left behind of how humanity lived. In European philosophy Hegel articulates a powerful characterisation of Africa as devoid of any history and merely a wasteland filled with lawlessness and cannibalism. Therefore, the African is:

The negro . . . [who] exhibits the natural man in his completely wild and untamed state. We must lay aside all thought of reverence and morality – all that we call feeling – if we would rightly comprehend him; there is nothing harmonious with humanity to be found in this type of character. (1956:93)

The defamation of Africa and African people in terms of their lack of human consciousness and humanity provides the justification for missionaries to enter Africa to impose order and education. Hegel's discourse on race focused upon two central claims: first, that Africa was a land with no past (in other words, the dehistoricising of African existence), second, along the same lines, Hume and Kant characterised African people as incapable of rational thought or ethical conduct. The defamation of Africa began with the assertion that the childish condition of Africans can be attributed to the geographical region in which they lived. According to Hegel, sub-Saharan Africa was a 'land of childhood' that lies 'beyond the day of self conscious history' (Hegel, 1956:91). Hegel's claims of geographical determinism proposed that Africans had not evolved to a condition of self-consciousness. He suggests that the Africans cut off from the world by mountain barriers displayed 'the most reckless inhumanity and barbarism,' and yet, like children, 'when their rage was spent, in the calm time of peace, they showed themselves mild and well disposed toward the Europeans, when they became acquainted with them' (Hegel, 1956:92).

Hegel develops a romantic ideal of the ignoble savage. A recurrent theme in the discourse of Hume, Kant and Hegel is the depiction of Africans as incapable of human thought, particularly the concept of the universal. According to Hegel, without a 'distinction between himself as an individual and the universality of his essential being . . . the Knowledge of an absolute Being, an Other, and a Higher than his individual self, is entirely wanting' (1956:93).

The 'savage' African becomes the justification for enslavement. He regards Africans as having 'perfect contempt for humanity which in its being on Justice and morality is the fundamental characteristic of the race' (1956:95). Hegel excuses the European enslavement of Africans by proposing that freedom's evolution is a slow process in human history. Only mature humans can attain consciousness of freedom. This maturation can take place only through the process of enslavement itself. He propounds:'slavery is in and for itself injustice, for the essence of humanity is Freedom; but for this man must be matured' (1956:99).

Africans who do not go through the maturation process cannot come to the human condition. The construction of Africans as outside the realm of humanity provided the 'way out' of possible moral inconsistencies such as the equality of all men and the dignity of persons enshrined within the philosophy of modernity. How could these moral ideals of universal humanity be reconciled with enslavement and colonial projects? The writings of Hume, Kant and Hegel presented a powerful and influential socially constructed discourse on race and in so doing 'Europe was able to posit and represent itself and its contingent historicity as the ideal culture, the ideal humanity and ideal history' (Eze, 1998:218).

Lesser-known philosophers such as Beattie (1770) challenged Hume's suggestion that 'all other species of men . . . [are] naturally inferior to whites'. According to Beattie (1770) the Africans and Americans (Native Americans) had arts and sciences that the Europeans could not imitate. He rejected the perceived inferiority assigned to Africans and indigenous peoples and opposed enslavement, referring to the condition of the slave as 'not favourable to genius of any kind' (1770:36). Enlightenment thinkers such as Beattie rejected a racial hierarchy of humanity, and European travellers who had encountered Africa themselves also presented a different account of Africans. For example, Count Constantin de Volney, a Frenchman (1757–1820) travelled to Egypt in the eighteenth century, prior to the invasion of the French Army, and claimed in his book, *Ruins of Empire* that Europe owed its arts, civilisations, and sciences to Africans. He writes: 'Just think that this race of black men, today our slave and the object of our scorn, is the very race to which we owe our arts, sciences, and even the use of speech!'

The dilemmas presented in the moral ideals of Enlightenment and modernity and their role in sustaining slavery and the subjugation of indigenous peoples through colonialism and imperialism requires further examination. The dominance of European thought as the universal norm has often served to cloak and negate the prospect of an examination of its cultural precepts and social formations and interests. However, Ani (1994) presents a powerful critique of European cultural thought and behaviour. Ani's (1994) analysis of European culture, thought and social behaviour processes contributes to an understanding of the way in which enslavement could be rationalised and points out the dilemmas inherent in the moral ideals of modernity and the enslavement and subjugation of indigenous peoples. Moreover, Ani (1994) proposes that the differential classification of humanity characterised by modernity and its role in the conquest and subjugation of indigenous peoples may be related to the imbalance of the feminine and masculine principles. The unequal power relationship between the male and female, coupled with the invention of hierarchical racial categories of humanity, provided the basis for defining the social positions of subjugated groups.

From an African-centred viewpoint, Ani (1994) describes three interrelated cultural components, the *asili*, *utamaroho* and *utamawazo* and helps us to understand their construction and functioning. The *asili* is described as the developmental seed of the culture, the *logos* that emanates from the culture. The *utamaroho* is the energy force of the culture, the *ethos*, as it motivates the collective attitude, reaction and behaviour of the culture. Finally, the *utamawazo* refers to cultural thought structure, the construction of thought and beliefs, which inform the functioning of the culture and are informed by the culture. Both the *utamaroho* and the *utamawazo* are born out of and are manifestations of the *asili*, and in turn affirm and strengthen it, providing an important cyclical cultural process.

Culture is understood as ideological 'since it possesses the force and power to direct activity, to mould personalities and to pattern behaviour' (Ani. 1994:5). European cultural components are characterised by domination and the 'will to power': that is, power over something/someone else that originates from *asili*. The *utamawazo* (the cultural thought structure) is based upon the dichotomies of mind/body; spirit/material; reason/emotion; intellect/nature; and individual/community. The philosophy of Enlightenment and modernity embraced the belief in, and supremacy of, the 'abstract', a detachment of thought, rationalism and scientism that involves an objectification of the 'other' as the ways and means of knowing. Ani (1994) argues that this rationale of dichtomisation contributes to a despiritualised concept of the universe and a culture based on materialism. The concept of self in European social thought is constructed as white, male, rational, scientific, civilised, conqueror and saviour. This construction denotes the power relationship over the European image of others as object, 'other', savage, primitive, backward, non-human. Lastly, the *utamaroho*, the energy force of culture, has driven political, cultural and intellectual imperialism. Modernity produced the use of 'scientism' as universal and objective ways of knowing and being in the world that are actually European culturally-specific, in contrast to a common understanding (shared by peoples of the world of Africa, Native Americas, Oceania and Asia) of the spiritual base of reality. There is rationalism and pragmatism within these worldviews, but these epistemologies do not dominate.

The legacy of modernity in researching black families

While this is perhaps a brief and simplified sketch of the complexities involved in the project of modernity, it is possible to identify philosophical, social and political orientations that have shaped and defined epistemologies in conventional social science knowledge production. Scheurich and Young (1997:7) have provided a well-informed exposition of racial bias in research epistemologies. They believe modernism 'is an epistemological, ontological and axiological network or grid that "makes" the world as the dominant western culture knows and sees it'. In this way, the dominant group creates reality in its own image through its socio-historical and economic experiences and, in so doing, the dominant culture creates and constructs the 'others' (Said, 1979; Hill-Collins, 1991). It is in the construct of the 'other' that modernity has framed underlying assumptions of analysis in the conventional conceptual models of black families. This is apparent in the universal application of concepts and methods set out for all families. As a consequence of this process, research analysis of black families has used comparative instruments to formulate frameworks that have often produced distortions about the lives of black people (Stanfield, 1985; Hill-Collins, 1991; Anderson, 1993). In short, these distortions 'dwell on the pathological and on the sensational' (Stanfield, 1985:411).

For example, the study by Gill and Jackson (1983) gives an example of the ways in which a comparative framework of analysis distorted the value systems and aspirations of black families. The study used a variety of qualitative research methods, semi-structured interviews, and questionnaires on health and social adjustment; in addition, concepts such as self-esteem were measured. The 36 families interviewed all included black children in transracial placements.

The areas of research covered relationships within the family, school peer groups, child's identity, experience of being 'coloured' and being adopted. Gill and Jackson (1983:130) concluded that 'these black children have been made white in all but skin colour . . . have no contact with the black community and their "coping" mechanisms are based on denying their racial background'. These conclusions are illustrated throughout the study, and here is an example of black child of mixed parentage describing herself: 'I suppose, I'd describe myself as medium height, I mean you know. Well, I suppose I could say I was white' (Gill and Jackson, 1983:73).

Gill and Jackson (1983:132) interpret their research findings by advising that 'they feel confident in using the term "success" to describe the experiences of the majority of these families and children'. This study raises a number of important questions, the first of which is their failure to recognise the identity needs of black children and the importance of those to their psychological wellbeing. Maxime (1993) draws attention to the significance of this issue because she argues that there are fewer opportunities for black children to experience nurturing and support for black identities and affirmation of self in wider society. Moreover, conventional theoretical concepts of identity formation tend to focus upon periphery factors such as the influence of school, parents and peer groups in individualised arenas, whereas African-centred orientations propose the formation of identity emerging through collective meanings within groups and communities (Graham, 1999).

The second area of critique is located in the value base and criteria of what constitutes 'success' in transracial placements. In this study, success was interpreted as meaning how far the black child had been assimilated into the white family. From a black perspective, this interpretation is misguided and assimilation represents not success but failure.

The study highlights the problems of applying a research model framed in a conventional conceptual model to black families. This framework firmly supported notions of assimilation as the measurement of success. This study had important repercussions for social work policy and practice. During this period, black professionals and community activists were involved in promoting and encouraging the recruitment of black parents as foster carers and adopters. This study undermined these initiatives in its support for the one-way traffic of black children into white families. Social research was used to prove the 'success' of this widespread social work policy and practice. Black professionals voiced their concerns in critical reviews of the methodology and interpretations of research findings in this study (J. Small, 1984).

English (1974) has provided a comprehensive review of sociological literature featuring studies of black families from the 1920s to the 1960s which indicate a clear parallel between black family research, social problems, social disorganisation and social pathology. The 'pathology' of black families was given the 'authenticity' of scientific social research.

Sociological literature and research concerned itself primarily with social problems and deviancy during the 1960s and 1970s: for example, the rising divorce rate, single parent families, homelessness, race relations, crime and immigration (Worsley, 1973). Black families were drafted into the 'social problems and deviancy' areas of sociological concerns (Phoenix, 1988). The heightened interest in black families fitted neatly into discourse on race relations and immigration and the perceived problematic nature of the black presence in British society. Thus these factors spearheaded intense research, discussion and debate about the nature of black family structure and functioning during the 1960s and 1970s.

Goldberg (2000) suggests that this intense research activity is directed towards the accumulation of knowledge about the racialised 'other' as the object of study. Moreover, through this process racialised knowledge can be socially managed as the 'other' is suppressed into silence. Goldberg (2000:155) describes the ways in which the environment of the 'other', 'the colonies . . . the prisons, ghettos and crowded inner cities became the laboratory in which these epistemological constructs [could] be tested'. The one-dimensional examination of the lives of minoritised communities prompted Stokely Carmichael (Carmichael and Hamilton, 1968:174) to call upon social scientists to 'stop investigating and examining people of colour and examine their own corrupt society'.

The debates and discussions surrounding black families have focused upon important issues of racism, race relations, social competence, socialisation, the effects of enslavement, identity, African retentions, strengths, colonialism, poverty and class (Moynihan, 1965; Rainwater, 1970; R. Hill, 1972; English, 1974; McAdoo, 1981; Nobles, 1985). These studies reveal two distinct approaches to the analyses of black family structures and functioning (Karenga, 1993): in the first, black family structures and functioning are inherently dysfunctional, which in turn produces dysfunctional members of society; the second approach emphasises black families' strengths and adaptive vitality.

A dysfunctional model of black families was cited in Moynihan (1965), in his report on 'the Negro family – the case for national action in the USA.'

He perceived black families as 'broken and unstable', and describes their functioning as a 'tangle of pathology'. He concluded that 'problem behaviours' were an integral part of a black lifestyle that perpetuated dysfunction without societal oppression. In a similar vein, enslavement is often cited as the main cause of social disorganisation within black families. Driver (1982) felt that the primacy of matrilineal households within black family structures was the direct result of enslavement due to the inevitable breakdown of family structures and functioning. The economic effects of high unemployment amongst black men compounded the dysfunctional attributes of black families. This approach to black family research has its parallels in Britain where the transference of deficit models into social science literature reveals another dimension to the debate. This dimension assumes the ideology of assimilation and integration. Denney (1983) explains the pathological model of black families in anthropological terms, evoking the locus of change that needs to take place within black families themselves. Similarly, Sheila Patterson's (1963) study, entitled *Dark Strangers*, which represents the post-war image and characterisation of black people as 'immigrants', applies a 'scientific' rationale to assess the process of adjustment and assimilation of black people into the British way of life. This study is couched within a framework of assimilation and the acceptance of 'immigrants' by the host society. The onus is upon black 'immigrants' to assimilate. Success is meaured by the varying degrees of assimilation and acculturation in the social realities of black family life. The framework of assimilation theories imposed upon black families belies the fact that there has been a continuous black presence in Britain for over 500 years.

Fitzherbert (1967) attributed the over-representation of black children in the public care system as being in part due to a tradition of unstable families. Cashmore (1979) and Pryce (1979) represented black families as weak and unstable, taking the view that black parents failed to take responsibility for their children or to supervise their young people. Black families were perceived as either imposing too much discipline or being too permissive. In any event, black families failed to utilise the socialising process in child-rearing so that their children could not accept or make use of 'correct' norms and values of society. The absence of the male presence was perceived as a contributory factor to the 'dysfunctional' black family and was related to the crime rates among young black men and teenage pregnancy in young women (Gilroy, 1982; S. Hall et al., 1982). Again, Mercer (1984:25) highlights the relationship between the growth of interest in research on black families as the primary locus of social pathology, the cycle of deprivation and the culture of poverty.

These conceptual models of black families entered theoretical models of social work and were exemplified in the policies and practices of social workers. For example, inertia surrounding the recruitment of black foster carers and adopters in the 1960s and 1970s resulted in the one-way traffic of black children placed with white foster carers and adopters. Similarly, distortions in the assessment process sometimes resulted in the inappropriate removal of black children by social workers (J. Small, 1984; V. Harris, 1991).

A closely associated model of black families cited in social science literature sees oppression and disadvantage as the key component of family structures and functioning. This approach considers the racial discrimination and oppression experienced by black families in many aspects of their lives. It is through their experience of discrimination that social problems are created and in turn become part of black family life. This theory contends that black families are at varying stages of assimilation although they ultimately share the same value system and worldviews as European families, and therefore their difference is centred upon their experience of discrimination and oppression (Liebow, 1967). These theories were popular in the 1970s and early 1980s and permeated many theoretical discussions in social work. This model was widely accepted because it served a useful purpose in acknowledging the impact of racism and oppression in black people's lives. However, this model raises problematics that place black families within a thematic parameter of victims whose lives are embedded and directed in reaction to and in response to racism. This general pathologising is grounded in the centrality of Eurocentrism in theories, perspectives and dynamics of social work.

Numerous black scholars and researchers mounted a critical appraisal of the preponderance of deficit models of black families in social science literature (Billingsley, 1968; R. Hill, 1972; English, 1974; Nobles, 1985). As a result of this process, black scholars have been engaged in time-consuming endeavours, refuting questionable theories and research findings, and neutralising distorted interpretations in academic scholarship. These efforts have been framed by an emphasis upon the strengths and adaptive vitality of black families. This approach considers the socio-economic effects of racism in the lives of black families. However, in this context the adaptive abilities and vitality of black families that emerge in response to the socio-economic effects of racism and oppression are not perceived as pathological, but as strengths (Billingsley, 1968; Staples, 1974; Nobles, 1978, 1985; Karenga, 1993). These strengths and abilities must be acknowledged and enhanced in the design and practice of helping interventions. In recent years this approach has been embraced by social work and has formed the basis for theories of empowerment (Solomon, 1976; Cloke and Davies, 1995). Initial responses to the strengths approach brought black families into discussions and debates about identifying and understanding the nature of their strengths and the ways in which social work can support capacity building inherent in these models. It is argued that these identified strengths have shown durability in the face of severe oppression and a history of dehumanisation and cultural degradation.

Whilst this model seeks to redress the balance in understanding the strengths and weaknesses in family structures and functioning, many black academics and professionals in the field have voiced their concern about some aspects of the strengths model (Cress-Wesling, 1973; English, 1974; Nobles, 1985; Bryan, 1992). These concerns centre upon questions of validity of strengths against the background of the dehumanising experience of oppression faced by many black families in Western societies. It is within this context that English (1974:40) examines the strengths of the family approach, which he believes 'helps make it easier for an oppressive society to ignore the heinous conditions it imposes on the black family'. Elsewhere this point is reiterated powerfully by Mercer (1984:25):

concerned liberal practitioners have responded by seeking to praise the black family's strengths; rather than malign it they have sought to support it to enable the black family to 'cope' with racism. But despite (or is it because of) their best intentions these notions cannot serve to enhance the interests of black people because they ignore and refuse to challenge, theoretically and practically, the actual conditions of the black family in a racist society.

Bearing this in mind, the strengths model poses serious dilemmas for black scholars, researchers and professionals. How do you prove strengths in oppression without diluting or drawing attention away from the dehumanising effects of racism and the oppressive nature of institutional racism? Nobles (1985) suggests that from a black perspective arguments may be advanced which propose that there no true positives under subjugated circumstances.

The definition of what constitutes strengths/positives has been defined by the dominant society and the understanding of black families remains immersed within a Eurocentric framework of research methodology. Therefore, black scholars have argued that no balanced appraisal of black family structure and functioning can take place (Akbar, 1985; Nobles, 1985; Asante, 1987; Graham, 1999). Moreover, the strengths approach has emerged in reaction to and in response to the negative valuations heaped upon black families within the social pathological and deviant models prevalent within social science literature. Critical black scholars have been mindful of attempts on the part of the oppressed to build a science of liberation contingent upon using the ideas and beliefs of oppressors, as this may contribute further to the legitimisation of oppression (Nobles, 1978; Semaj, 1996). As Nobles (1976:173) maintains:

> *as long as black researchers ask the same questions and theorise in the same theory as their white counterparts, black researchers will continue to be part and parcel of the system which perpetuates the misunderstanding of black reality and consequently contributes to our degradation.*

The strengths of black families initially identified by black scholars and researchers have since been evaluated further as *characteristics rather than strengths* inherent in black families, and these characteristics provide a resource to generate knowledge for social work practice. In this way, agency is restored to black families and communities. This is because critical analysis takes place within a matrix of African-centred approaches to understanding family structures and functioning (Akbar, 1976).

Conclusion

In this chapter I have explored the philosophical and social underpinnings of social work knowledge. Although this field is a broad terrain, I have attempted to link social work's philosophical foundations that are implicated in creating the conditions of exclusion and racial hierarchy. These contingencies are in stark contrast to social work's mission to bring about equality and social justice. Therefore, it is necessary for social workers to examine the ways in which Eurocentric philosophical precepts and suppositions in the representations of the 'other' are infused into racialised discourses and enter social work theory and practice.

Attention has been given to the obstacles for social work in bringing about a more equitable society based on principles of social justice. However, an in-depth understanding of the philosophical assumptions inherent in knowledge for social work may shed light on its propensity to create conditions for inequality and oppression. Moreover, an examination of the underpinnings of modern day social work practice can enhance our understanding of contemporary conceptual approaches and in this way examine them more critically. As a consequence of the limitations identified in the foundations of existing social work, and in accordance with social work principles of equality and humanitarian values, these insights call for a philosophical diversification to spearhead social change. This approach invites an expansion of conceptual frameworks to promote equality of worldviews and their validity in social work theory and practice.

Chapter 3
An African heritage in the development of social welfare

Traditionally, the social hierarchies of class and gender have been the main targets of critical social welfare discourse. These areas of study represent important lines of inquiry and accounts of the hierarchical bonds of class and gender in the formation and development of social welfare institutions. However, what is clearly missing is an account of the ideological constructions of race and their entrance into the broad spectrum of welfare philosophies shaping the development of welfare institutions. Although Sudbury (1997:165) quite rightly observes that 'British racism is shaped by a history of slavery which retained the majority of enslaved Africans at a physical distance from the majority of British beneficiaries of slavery', the black presence during a critical phase in the development of social welfare has been largely ignored. As a result of this process, the black presence has generally been confined to post-war race relations analyses.

These omissions in the history of social welfare are symptomatic of the 'invisible man' syndrome prevalent in the mainstream texts on the history of Britain (Ellison, 1965). The recent upsurge of interest in the history of black people has been largely confined to a small group of academics. Why has the African heritage been severed and its contemporary relevance ignored? This question challenges the decisive ways in which knowledge has evolved within and through the delineated boundaries of colonialisation. These cultural frames of reference have created the conditions that serve to sever the historical connections that bind people of African descent to an African heritage in social welfare.

The construct of social welfare texts framed within delineated stages of recent time draws attention to the ways in which a dehistorisation process shapes and defines Western knowledge discourses and is an inherent 'part of the colonialist and imperial project on Africa' (Dei, 1999c:6). The reading of the histories of colonialised peoples strictly within the time frame of colonialisation conspires to suppress the need for people to affirm subject accounts of their histories and cultures.

Lewis (2000) identifies several approaches to race and ethnicity ascribed in the directions of social relations. First, it is implied that the relations between black and white people are a post-1945 phenomenon. Second, a race relations 'problem' is linked to questions of immigration juxtaposed to the improvement of race relations and multiculturalism. Third, the 'problems' of minoritised communities are caused by external contingencies that lead to 'internal' problems located largely in inner cities where minoritised communities reside. This approach brings to the fore the constructs in which 'amnesia' characterises contemporary social welfare literature.

Lewis (2000:265) uses the term 'forgettings' as persistent and active to describe events in historical times that are omitted. She argues that these elements 'have made it possible to construct the issue of race as an "externally" generated issue – "external" in the double sense of neither originating within the territory of the UK, nor as endemic to the internal (domestic or imperial) politics and trajectory of the UK'.

In contrast to this approach, an anti-colonial stance breaks away from the practice of basing knowledge exclusively on the experience of colonialisation and its aftermath towards an epistemology of the colonised anchored within a sense of collective consciousness (Dei, 1999c). In this context, a sense of historical continuity is preserved and thereby assists in cultivating an understanding of the relationships and parallels between the past and the present. These historical understandings assist in the rupture of conventional discourse where 'the oppressed group's own experience and interpretation of social life finds little expression that touches the dominant culture, while the same culture imposes on the oppressed group its experience and interpretation of social life' (Young, 1990:60). The process of decolonisation maintains the importance and exposition of cultural resource knowledge and 'sees marginalised groups as subjects of their own experiences and histories' (Dei, 1999c:10). This approach chimes with the process and goals of empowerment in social work.

Empowerment has its basis in self-help activities, traditions of mutual aid and human and civil rights social movements (Simon, 1990). Lee (1994:40) contends that empowerment implies a heightened critical consciousness tethered to a sense of peoplehood. She advocates that the learning of a group's history of oppression is an important part of the development of 'critical understandings in ourselves and in our clients'. Therefore, 'social workers must develop a historic and longitudinal view' because the need for empowerment is rooted in historic and contemporary racism and cultural disparagement of subjugated groups. A group's history of oppression brings to the fore a foundation of the empowerment process in establishing an explication of 'hidden' histories.

44

These 'hidden' histories can reveal the source of the inequities and short-comings of contemporary social welfare and assist in identifying patterns of discrimination that have infiltrated the instruments of social welfare. Moreover, empowering communities requires an appreciation of historical and contemporary helping processes and a sense of the ways in which cultural knowledge and one's humanity can bring about experiences of freedom and liberation from oppressive barriers and control.

Social welfare perspectives have an important part to play in not only enhancing direct social service provision but also in providing a critical under-standing of the economical, social and political realities that shape and define policy interventions. Critical understanding of social welfare perspectives can assist social workers by informing their styles of practice and their actions. This approach to critical understanding can be developed in various ways.

First, knowledge about social policies and inequities that have arisen must necessarily be approached from a societal context. In this way, the use of history can provide the vehicle for understanding and appreciating the broader context in which social work evolved and the structural causes of inequalities. Social welfare history brings to the fore institutional barriers created largely by philosophical underpinnings, representations, beliefs and ideas that served as a critical intermediary between individual and family wellbeing and instruments of government.

Second, social welfare history can assist in understanding the contours of contemporary social policy considerations, in particular the economic and political contingencies and their impact upon recipients of welfare. These meanings of welfare define the various ways in which social services are developed and managed. In Britain, social work operates largely within a general system of social welfare provision, which has considerable influence in shaping and directing social work practice. In recent times there have been profound changes and shifts in forms of welfare provision. These shifts reflect different political approaches to welfare and the complex changes in social conditions and welfare expectations that have taken place across social, political and economic domains. In this context, key characteristics of welfare have been challenged, bringing forth a restructuring and new approach to welfare. These dynamics have directed and shaped new thinking about social work, its priorities and professional practice.

Exploring an African heritage in social welfare

The experience of the enslavement of African people and its legacy and impact on social welfare have been well documented in the USA and elsewhere within the diaspora, yet have remained unacknowledged until now in the history of British social welfare (Billingsley and Giovannoni, 1972). In addition, the African presence provides an opportunity to explore social welfare among a group of people endeavouring to improve their lives, starting from a baseline of enslavement and servitude. In this context, the enslaved and 'free' African community living in Britain in the eighteenth-century provides a unique area of study that raises important questions concerning the nature of deep-seated racism, its impact and shaping of welfare considerations.

The African presence was first recorded during the Roman occupation around 210 AD when African soldiers formed an important contingent in the Roman army. Historians have provided compelling evidence to support assertions of a consistent permanent black community in Britain for at least the past 500 years (Banton, 1972; Shyllon, 1977a; Fryer, 1984; Walvin, 1994).

The African heritage in the development of social welfare can be found deep in the recesses of British history and immersed within the layers of welfare ideology characterised by the hierarchical bonds of class, gender and race. The prevailing ideology of *laissez-faire* in nineteenth-century Britain generated notions of the deserving and undeserving, the adequate and inadequate, the inferior and superior, moral and immoral. Drawing upon the preceding chapter, these ways of separating and evaluating humanity can be traced to the philosophies of the Enlightenment. Thus, the Enlightenment produced a powerful striving for classification, fragmentation and binary opposites, and played a central role in codifying and institutionalising scientific perceptions of the human race (Eze, 1997).

The biological invention of race and its pseudo-scientific construction entered the academic and intellectual world of European scholars and politicians in the 1700s (Stocking, 1982; Fryer, 1984; Bernal, 1987). Thus the prevailing vision of social welfare gave rise to a view of social hierarchies as inevitable and natural and so provided the basis for justifying the institution of enslavement.

During the sixteenth, seventeenth and eighteenth centuries, Britain was inextricably involved in one of the major tragedies of human history, the enslavement and murder of millions of African people. The term Maafa – a Kiswahili term meaning disaster – is often used to describe the forced abduction of African people across the Atlantic, the 'middle passage' to the Caribbean, the Americas and England (Richards, 1980). Contrary to popular belief, African people, men, women and children were enslaved in Britain, bought and sold as chattels or commodities, a fact validated by numerous advertisements of the period (Shyllon, 1977a; Fryer, 1984; Lorimer, 1992).

The growing African community in London during the 1700s consisted of enslaved and some 'free' African people. One historian, Shyllon (1977), notes that until 1772 most African people were enslaved except for some 'free' African people who evaded recapture. The population of African people was estimated to be in the region of 10 – 15,000 (Shyllon, 1974). According to Banton (1972), towards the end of the eighteenth century, 2 per cent of the population were people of African descent. The majority of enslaved African population consisted of children and young people, a pattern reflected within the enslaved populations in the Americas and the Caribbean (N. Myers, 1993; Braidwood, 1994).

The community also included African people who had arrived after enlisting to fight for Britain during the American War of Independence, for which they were promised their freedom (Gerzina, 1995). These African soldiers made claims for compensation for losses that they incurred in the same way as their British counterparts but their claims were mostly rejected. The Government declared that as the soldiers had 'gained their liberty' in the war 'instead of being sufferers [these men] had no right to ask for or expect anything from the Government – applications hardly deserve serious answer' (Shyllon, 1977a:121). These conditions precipitated the context in which these men were forced into abject poverty and mostly resorted to begging on the streets of London. For example, Peter Anderson, a Virginia woodcutter, offers a description of the sort of poverty and destitution which many African soldiers experienced.

I endeavour'd to get work but cannot get any I am thirty nine years of age and am ready and willing to service his Britanack majesty while I am able but I am realy starvin about the streets, having nobody to give me a morsal of bread and dare not go home to my own country again. (quoted in Fryer, 1984:194)

Peter Anderson was awarded £10 after receiving help from Lord Dunmore to verify his claim. However, this award was exceptional and 'by mid 1786 there were at the very least 1,444 of them living in London, and most were penniless' (Fryer, 1984:194).

There are further examples of institutional racism and obstacles set in place to thwart attempts by enslaved and 'free' Africans to access social welfare. The principle of public responsibility for the poor and needy was already established in the Poor Law of 1601 that introduced the first modern form of public social welfare. The Poor Law established notions of the 'deserving poor' and 'undeserving poor' that reflected the social beliefs and attitudes of the eighteenth and nineteenth centuries where poverty was a sign of moral weakness and personal inadequacy (Bolt, 1971).

Many destitute African people who sought poor relief could not meet the criteria of settlement. The Act of Settlement 1662 decreed that those not possessing property, living outside their parish and not able to give an assurance that they would never become a charge upon the parish, could be removed to their native parish in which they had settlement and which was legally obliged to provide relief in cases of need.

Settlement rights could be acquired in a number of ways; birth, marriage, apprenticeship or one year's continuous employment within a given parish. For African people who had acquired their 'freedom', the Act of Settlement not only placed institutional barriers in the way of applying for poor relief but located such African people in a precarious and vulnerable position as undeserving poor or outside the system of poor relief altogether. The following is a brief summary of the obstacles constructed by racist ideologies which thwarted attempts by black communities to access poor relief.

First, the majority of black people had no parish of settlement. The 'free' Africans could not return to their homeland to experience yet again the barbarism and cruelty of enslavement even if they managed to survive the horrors of the 'middle passage'. Second, settlement acquired through apprenticeship employment was forbidden through an order issued by the Lord Mayor of London in 1731 'that for the future no negroes or other blacks be suffered to be bound Apprentices at any companies of this City' (Fryer, 1984:74).

Third, evidence from the narratives of African people themselves indicates that their endeavours to obtain employment were severely hampered by widespread racism, discrimination and oppression. For example, a narrative written by Ottobah Cugoano in Britain in 1791 describes the difficulties in finding employment and observes that 'complexion is a predominant prejudice for a man to starve for want in a Christian country' (Edwards and Dabydeen, 1991:53). Fourth, enslaved African people were not even given the status of 'pauper' and found themselves outside the relief system altogether. They earned no wages as their labour was given 'freely' as an integral part of their enslavement. For example, the case of Charlotte Howe, an enslaved African woman, demonstrates the ways in which the institution of enslavement determined the status of black people and as a consequence placed them outside legal remedies. Charlotte Howe met the requirements of settlement (that is, one year's continual residence and work); however, she received no wages as an enslaved person and therefore could not be in employment and was ineligible for poor relief (Lorimer, 1992).

In this context, N. Myers, (1993:53) holds that the black community's difficulties in accessing poor relief placed them in a precarious position. The law consistently ruled that enslaved black people were not hired servants and therefore not entitled to wages, and as a result of these judgements they 'failed to be cushioned by the safety net of poor relief'.

These experiences of racism grounded in the contours of early social welfare demonstrate the ways in which enslaved and 'free' African people elicited different responses from the state and instruments of welfare.   In these cases their attempts to access social welfare were firmly linked to their status as 'property', and they were not entitled to any amelioration of their circumstances. Historically, for most black people racism and oppression became the source of injustice and discrimination throughout their lives.

Models of enslavement and connections with the development of social welfare

The nineteenth century represented a period of industrial expansion, the advent of capitalist economics, and the establishment of social hierarchy based upon social class, gender and race.The nature and purpose of social welfare was dominated by a *laissez-faire* economics that supported the primacy of individualism within the social order.

Laissez-faire ideology provided the moral foundations for social welfare and the Poor Law and shaped attitudes towards poverty and destitution. Poverty was associated with 'sin and slothfulness', being a sign of moral weakness and personal inadequacy (Bolt, 1971). The continuing prevalence of widespread poverty stimulated public and political discussions about the need to develop social welfare.

Laissez-faire ideology, manifested in the oppressive nature of the Poor Laws, generated notions of the deserving and undeserving poor, the adequate and the inadequate, the inferior and the superior, the moral and immoral. Its configurations provide the most salient expression of racial supremacy embedded within modernity. The influence of enslavement in British social welfare provides insights into the lasting effects of racism that continue to be 'transmitted...through institutions, public and private, from decade to decade, from generation to generation down three and half centuries to the present harsh reality' (Stuckey, 1996:108).

In order to present a cogent exploration of the connections between enslavement and social policy, I propose four models of enslavement that have influenced the instruments of social welfare during a critical period in the development of the modern welfare state:

- enslavement as a model of destitution
- enslavement as a model of social welfare
- enslavement as a model of salvation
- enslavement as a model of social exclusion

Enslavement as a model of destitution
The rise of industrialisation during the nineteenth century required that poor children should work long hours in deplorable conditions in factories throughout Britain. Poor and abandoned children were placed in workhouses under the Poor Law or put out into apprenticeships until they reached the age of 21 years. Social historians have documented the appalling conditions of poor children in factories, mines, workhouses and as parish apprentices (George, 1987). As the notion of childhood slowly emerged, reformers campaigned for state intervention in the form of legislation to bring about the end of child labour. So began a critical period of reform when the impact of enslavement produced important considerations in the history of child welfare.

Ideologies of enslavement, whether pro or anti, were premised upon the notion that the African was inferior, most often childlike, with a characteristic trait of absolute helplessness, 'beset with immense perils; their very freedom being a powerful temptation to idleness, disaffection and violence' (Leeds Freedmen's Aid Society, 1865). These representations of African people can be traced to Hegel's philosophical writings in which he expressed the widely held views of European explorers, missionaries, colonisers and others (Outlaw, 1996).

Burton (1998) argues that feminists relied upon the general identification with the 'slave' to validate their quest for political emancipation and in order to participate in the imperial civilising mission. The narrative of abolition encompassed a pro-empire identity that enveloped images of the African as a savage, helpless victim so that 'the imperial mother ... bestows the blessings of freedom, Christianity and western civilisation on her enslaved colonial offspring' (Midgley, 1992:205).

The anti-slavery movement presented images of enslaved Africans as objects of pity including extreme human degradation and appalling destitution: 'no such absolutely pauper population has probably ever been known in modern times' (Leeds Freedmen's Aid Society, 1865, cited in Bolt, 1971). The institution of enslavement and the campaign for its abolition became enmeshed in the movement for legislative and social welfare reform. Contemporaneously, the prevalent images of working-class children as victims of cruelty, neglect, hunger, homelessness and indifference spearheaded a 'range of child rescue operations particularly in London in the 1860s, 1870s, 1880s: child saving during this period was concerned with the resocialisation of children, aimed at their restoration from the residuum to the respectable working class' (Frost and Stein, 1989:28).

There are numerous examples of social reformers using the institution of enslavement to highlight the plight of poor white children:

much was said of black slaves and their chains; no doubt they were entitled to freedom, but were there no slaves except those of sable hue? ... [Mr. Grant] would name an instance of this kind of slavery which took place at Wigan. A child, not ten years of age ... thus burthened like a galley slave. (Grant, 1833 quoted in Royston and Pike, E, 1966).)

Mary Carpenter, an ardent campaigner for the abolition of slavery and social reformer, launched her first independent school for 'ragged children' in 1846. She linked the enslavement of African people to her mission on behalf of poor children in Bristol (Kendall, 1985).

Social reformers depicted Africans as childlike, primitive, slaves by nature passive degraded victims who came to represent the absolute model of extreme human degradation and destitution; a paradigm for the lowest level of poverty. Within the matrix of hierarchical conceptions of poverty, the institution of enslavement emerged as the social barometer providing a baseline in the treatment of English working-class children. The appalling treatment of poor working-class children could be rationalised by the notion that they were treated better than the enslaved African child. The ideology of race played a major role in perceiving people as 'races'. Race, as a European concept of human worth, emerged as a determining factor in the quality of life of individuals and communities. Thus, the English working-class child must rise above the enslaved African child so that the position of the European could be maintained within the ideological construction of racial hierarchy. Billingsley and Giovannoni (1972) suggest that, in the USA, the institution of enslavement which was codified and embedded within consti-tutional systems and social relations may have weakened the reforms for poor white children. However, I maintain it is difficult to develop a similar argument in the case of British social welfare, in part because of the small population of enslaved African children and also because of the limited entry of the codification of enslavement into the institutions of British society.

Enslavement as a model of social welfare

Billingsley and Giovannoni (1972) contend that until 1865 enslavement was the major social welfare institution for African children in the USA. DuBois (1935), a renowned black scholar, identified the peculiar ways in which the institution of enslavement performed social welfare functions in contrast to free labourers:

> *the Negroes were protected by a certain primitive sort of old age pensions, job insurance, sickness insurance; that is they must be supported in some fashion, when they were too old to work; they must have attention in sickness, for they represented capital; and they could never be among the employed.* (DuBois, 1935:9)

The majority of the enslaved African population consisted of children and young people, a pattern reflected within the enslaved populations in the Americas, the Caribbean and England (N. Myers, 1993; Braidwood, 1994). Enslavement and servitude were the hallmark of the first social welfare insti-tution for African children. Enslavement by its very nature constituted a form of extreme child cruelty. Unfortunately, very little is known about the lives of these enslaved children. The information available is mostly adult recollections in the form of narratives, which give shocking glimpses of the devastation of enslavement. The dearth of literature about the lives of enslaved children is mirrored in the studies of enslavement throughout the diaspora. Enslaved children did not have the opportunity to write or speak for themselves. They were forced to confront situations of terror, and witnessed or experienced horrific incidents of cruelty and barbarism at an early age (King, 1995). Olaudah Equiano, a leader of the African community living in

London during the eighteenth century, reflected upon his experience of enslavement as a young man: 'When you make men slaves you deprive them of half their virtue, you set them in your own conduct an example of fraud, rapine, and cruelty, and compel them to live with you in a state of war' (Equiano, 1794:75).

Equiano's view that enslavement was tantamount to a state of almost perpetual war reveals some insight into the fear, despair and misery experienced by African children. The enslaved African children in Britain constituted a unique group within the history of enslavement throughout the diaspora for two reasons. First, their experience of enslavement was characterised by separation from (or at least minimal contact with) enslaved adults. These children constituted a particularly vulnerable group, having no parents or adults to temper the harsh realities of enslavement. Enslaved African children learned very early on that their very survival was predicated upon the whims of their white 'masters', and most poignantly that their 'childhood was a common school in survival without power' (Huggins, 1990:171). Second, the use of African children as objects of fashion who could be treated as pets was widespread amongst the aristocracy and middle classes:

> *It was modish for ladies and gentlemen of fashion to keep 'negro' slaves. The ladies preferred small, plump faced boys who they dressed exotically and treated as 'pets'. They bought silver padlocks for them from Matthew Dyer in Duck Lane, Westminster who advertised (*London Advertiser 1756*), 'padlocks for blacks or dogs'. They named them Pompey and found them vastly more amusing than lapdogs.*
> (Mackenzie-Grieve, 1968:36)

The enslavement of African children remained an integral part of British society until the abolition of enslavement in 1834 and beyond.

Enslavement as a model of salvation

The religious philanthropic character of nineteenth century social welfare had a significant impact on the development of social welfare instruments, policy and practice. The Poor Law was closely involved with voluntary organisations and often the same group of people took part in the operation of both institutions. The voluntary societies were particularly influential in the shaping of child-care policy as well as the Poor Law itself (Hendrick, 1994).

In the latter part of the nineteenth century there was an expansion in the numbers of religious voluntary organisations involved in rescuing and saving the children of the poor 'from the immorality of his or her environment' (Hendrick, 1994:82). For example, Dr. Barnardos, National Childrens Home, the Catholic Crusade of Rescue and Church of England's Waifs and Strays Society mostly agreed on the central task of rescuing poor children. These organisations considered that poor families failed to provide moral and religious guidance to their offspring. The view of poverty as a sin and immoral propagated by the voluntary societies strengthened the belief that the cause of social problems lay in the individual rather than society. Thus, 'self-help and charity engendered virtue and the public purse produced vice' (Lees, 1998:88).

Jones (1994) identifies the comparisons made by General William Booth of the Salvation Army between the poor working class and African people in his work, *Darkest England, or The Way Out* (1890). Booth writes:

> *But while brooding over the awful presentation of life as it exists in the vast African forest, it seemed to me only too vivid a picture of many parts of our own land. As there is a darkest Africa, is there not also a darkest England? Civilisation, which can breed its own pygmies? May we not find a parallel at our own doors, and discover within a stone's throw of our cathedrals and palaces similar horrors to those....existing in the great Equatorial forest? (pp. 11–12)*

The institution of enslavement provided an ideal site for Christian evangelists and missionaries. Their religious doctrines embraced the view that Africans were heathens and sub-humans who were in need of a civilising mission. As Ani (1994:158) maintains:

> *the English slave trade, like that of other European nations, was launched with the blessings of the Church. It is ironic but not contradictory that the first English slaver was named 'Jesus' and that the first two rules Captain Hawkins imposed on his crew were, to serve God daily, and to love one another... There is no doubt that the Christian community gave its blessings to the slaving venture, participated in it and contributed to its success.*

The notion of the heathen African became closely allied with the institution of enslavement. Enslavement was considered a 'blessing' in order that the African could be 'saved' and civilised. M. Turner (1982) argues that many missionaries supported the institution of enslavement by co-operating with slave owners to focus upon the 'spiritual' aspects of enslaved Africans rather than entering into the dissolution of enslavement itself.

During the period between 1830 and 1870, when conversion fervour was at its height, Christianity and 'civilising' African people became inseparable (Curtin, 1965). Consequently, many enslaved African people believed that baptism conferred 'freedom' and some protection against possible recapture. Philanthropic activities drawn from religious and charitable organisations strengthened this view so that these attitudes and beliefs became enshrined as an integral part of their underlying value systems. Thus the institution of enslavement as a model of salvation supported Christian missionary zeal which was active in the shaping and conceptualisation of welfare within charitable organisations and the crossover into state institutions. These philosophies formed the basis of early social work theory and practice when professional social work emerged as an important social welfare institution.

Enslavement as a model of social exclusion

Social welfare institutions during the eighteenth and nineteenth centuries did not consider African people to be among the deserving poor; they were outside the system of poor relief or relegated to the status of the undeserving poor. The social welfare needs of African people were regarded as being satisfied through the institution of enslavement as chattels, or special property to be bought and sold. As Lorimer (1984:124) describes it:

> *blacks remained the only persons in English society liable to be treated as pieces of property. Newspaper advertisements for slaves, their sale at public auctions, and the offering of rewards for the capture of fugitives showed both an acceptance of the treatment of blacks as chattels and a toleration for the presumed property rights of masters.*

In the face of deep poverty and destitution black people resorted to begging on the streets of London. In response to the plight of the 'black poor', a committee was set up in 1786 by a group of philanthropists, businessmen and abolitionists, who raised money from public appeal to provide food, clothing and shelter. The donations were soon supplemented and taken over by the government and represented the first milestone in the access of social welfare by the African community. They joined the poor as a maligned group seen as a burden rather than objects of charity. The press and Parliament continued to express concern about the drain on the poor rate (Braidwood, 1994).

Public opinion demanded the removal of the 'black poor'. The policy of removal was consistent with the practice of sending Irish and Scottish paupers back to their homelands (Fraser, 1976). The black poor presented the government of the day with a dilemma in respect of the their 'free' status and growing public opinion demanding their removal from the shores of Britain. The committee recommended that the most effective way to remove the black poor permanently was to deport them. As a consequence of this recommendation a scheme of resettlement in Sierra Leone was devised. The committee introduced sanctions upon African people in an attempt to impose a requirement to join the scheme of settlement as a precondition for poor relief. The plan to deport the black poor was received with deep suspicion by African people. Cugoano, a leader of the black community, expressed his disquiet at the incongruity of a British government promoting a free settlement for the black poor as an act of charity yet also enslaving African people on the coast of West Africa (Braidwood, 1994). He explains that:

many more of the black people still in this country would have, with great gladness, embraced the opportunity, longing to reach their native land; but as the old saying is, A burnt child dreads the fire, some of these unfortunate sons and daughters of Africa have been severally unlawfully dragged away from their native abodes, under various pretences, by insidious treachery of others, and have been brought into the hands of barbarous robbers and pirates, and, like sheep to the market, have been sold into slavery. (quoted in Shyllon, 1977a:139)

The government yielded to public opinion and used various tactics to coerce African people to leave, including threats of arrest if found begging and being forcibly taken aboard ships to await deportation. As a result of this process the deportation of the black poor did not run smoothly. Many African people refused to go aboard ships commissioned for the crossing. The ships were not ready to sail and African men, women and children stayed aboard in deplorable conditions. Some died from fever while others tried to go ashore (Braidwood, 1994). *The Public Advertiser* (20 January 1787) reported on the group of black people seen on the streets of Plymouth:

the vessel not being ready to sail, [they] rambled about the streets, when by the severity of the cold, two of them dropt down dead; and the rest, had it not been for the humanity of the inhabitants, who gave them cloaths and necessaries, would have share, their likely unhappy fate. (Braidwood, 1994:146)

Eventually, the ships set sail for Sierra Leone with fewer than 400 African people on board. Some did not survive the journey; others died several months after landing in Sierra Leone. Some people were sold into enslavement. The Sierra Leone escapade was a failed attempt by the authorities to deport the black poor. However, the majority of African people stayed in Britain, continuing to eke out an existence and to survive the rigours of poverty and deep-seated racism in British society.

Affirming African humanity in the face of atrocity

An African heritage in social welfare reveals a legacy of black helping processes which originated in pre-colonial, ancient Africa, survived the experience of enslavement and continues to be found in black communities in post-war Britain (Martin and Martin, 1995; Graham, 1999; 2001). The enslaved African people brought with them a cultural value system that has its philosophical roots in the classical African civilisations of Kemet, Nubia, Kush and Axum (Diop, 1978; Williams, 1987; Asante, 1988; Asante and Abarry, 1995). These cultural ways of knowing can be traced to helping processes based on African social philosophies, reveal active components that include solidarity, mutuality, collective responsibility, spirituality, and reciprocity and community personhood (Dei, 1994). These paradigms seek to reclaim the wisdom, sacred traditions and invaluable helping skills that are grounded in cultural antecedents. Early examples of black responses to social need are located in efforts to secure the emancipation of African people during the 1700s. The institution of enslavement inadvertently reinforced black helping processes, providing the impetus for group solidarity which produced a sense of mutual aid and community solidarity.

There is very little direct testimony about the lives of enslaved or 'free' African people in Britain. N. Myers (1993) expresses concern about the reliance upon a few well-known figures in making assertions about the 'ordinary' lives of African people during enslavement. However, in the absence of this material, the narratives from formerly enslaved African people offers written proof of the protests and affirmation of African humanity in the face of atrocity. These qualitative materials provide confirmation of an African heritage expressed within the social practices and formations in black communities.

The context and source of African solidarity was inextricably bound up in and expressed within the resistance and self-emancipation of the African community. It is difficult to imagine successful leadership within the African community given the oppressive forces present in eighteenth-century Britain. Yet a group of African men calling themselves 'sons of Africa' emerged during the late eighteenth century as a potent force, possibly the first named African-centred political organisation in Britain. The sons of Africa included Olaudah Equiano, already known as a leader of the African community, Ottobah Cugoano, Broughwar Jogensmel, Yahne Aelane, Cojoh Ammere, George Mandeville, William Greek, Bernard Elliot Griffiths and Thomas Cooper (Shyllon, 1977a).

The sons of Africa set about planning ongoing resistance through mobilising the African community and establishing political and social gatherings. Olaudah Equiano published his narrative in 1789. His book became a best seller and preceded a lecture tour throughout Britain speaking on the evils of enslavement.

In 1787 Ottobah Cugoano also published his narrative with the help of Olaudah Equiano. Cugoano was forthright in his condemnation of enslavement and demanded the total freedom of African people. He also declared that African people had a moral duty to resist enslavement. Cugoano believed that every person in Britain was in some degree responsible for the enslavement of African people. The sons of Africa mounted a sustained campaign, writing to newspapers, publishing statements, lobbying Parliament and addressing meetings on the abolition of enslavement. The sons of Africa took part in many public debates: for example, on 7 May 1789, at the Coachmakers-Hall Society in London, a report of the debate proclaims:

> *several gentlemen with great ability reprobated the Slave Trade as totally repugnant to humanity, and the principles of a free country. One gentleman only opposed the abolition, which he did in a speech of great fluency and strength of reasoning. He was replied to by an African, (not Gustavus Vassa) who discovered much strong natural sense, and spoke with wonderful facility.* (Shyllon, 1977b:451)

The sons of Africa collaborated with each other, writing letters and narratives and working in the interests of the African community. They supported the community in their demands for wages for work and many enslaved Africans were able to 'buy' their freedom. They were active in the community, and used their influence to support their brothers and sisters in many ways, they also celebrated legal victories in the struggle against enslavement.

Fryer (1984) describes the visit of about 300 African people to support two black men who were imprisoned for the crime of begging; contributions were forthcoming from the community towards their upkeep during their confinement.

The sons of Africa became the focal point for news and information gathered from the dockside about rebellion and enslavement in the Caribbean and Americas. African people met whenever they could, sometimes in taverns, and they organised social gatherings to celebrate the victory of their kin, as Fryer (1984:69) reveals: 'a few days later this partial victory was celebrated by a gathering of about 200 blacks, "with their ladies", at a Westminster public house'. People held in high esteem others like themselves who sought to relieve suffering by drawing strength from their ancestral past.

As indicated earlier in this chapter, enslaved and 'free' African people experienced high levels of extreme poverty and destitution during the late eighteenth and nineteenth centuries. Amidst the ravages, poverty and deep-seated racism, the African community in London established 'clubs to support those who were "out of place" (Fryer, 1984:70). The term 'out of place' refers to those without employment, probably enslaved African people who had 'run away'. They were offered support and assistance. These early self-help groups within the African community provide evidence of a high level of solidarity and the expression of the principle within African philosophy of 'I am because we are', emphasising the interdependency of the individual and the group' (Mbiti, 1970:141).

Cultural antecedents inherent within various helping processes have guided, shaped and defined forms of resistance and social welfare efforts to ameliorate desperate social conditions and experiences of enslavement, destitution and racial oppression in Britain. These social practices set the thematic parameters of social welfare in black communities. The emphasis upon forms of mutuality and collective responsibility can be traced to African cultural and historical value systems as 'the expression of traditional African consciousness and morality' (Magdol, 1977:11). It was through the modality of mutual aid that black people engaged in an important form of resistance: survival (Carlton-LaNey, 1999).

Spirituality forms the cornerstone of African-centred worldviews and is the essence of human beings. Spirituality has been defined as 'the creative life-force, the very essence of all things' that connect all human beings to each other (Arewa, 1998:xvii). Spirituality has been one of the enduring features of African people; as Richards (1980:24) says 'the spirit of Africa was reborn in the form of [the] African...ethos' that helped them survive the chaos and trauma of enslavement.

There was a deep sense of kinship in pre-colonial Africa that African people took with them, expressed in a sense of self as part of a family and self as part of a community. Olaudah Equiano's (1794:85) well-known narrative expressed that deep sense of belonging to each other even under oppressive circumstances when he meets a young African child in the Isle of Wight: 'he soon came close to me, and caught hold of me in his arms as if I had been his brother, though we have never seen each other before'.

An African-centred paradigm places emphasis upon the collective nature of human beings and their group survival. This approach values the uniqueness of the individual but rejects the idea that the individual can be understood in isolation from others (Akbar, 1984).

The unfolding of hidden histories also provides the context in which black activism has shaped and defined some models of social welfare in black communities. These early forms of resistance to racism and oppression continued to be expressed in Pan-African organisations and groups at the beginning of the twentieth century. Fryer (1984:272) alludes to the importance of Pan-Africanism as a major political tradition of the twentieth century that 'was largely created by black people living in Britain'. Although the Pan-African movement was concerned with wider issues of colonialisation, imperialism racism and inequalities throughout the diaspora, they played a pivotal role in defending the rights of black people living in Britain. These struggles for a better and fairer society gave rise to concerns about the social and welfare needs of black people and their families in their efforts to forge greater self-determination.

Many organisations emerged during this period: for example, the African Progressive League, the African Children's Fund, the Coloured Seaman's Industrial League, The League of Coloured Peoples, and the Pan-African Federation. These organisations raised funds for various social welfare activities, held conferences, actively supported black rights, provided assistance for families in need, held family days, gave help in finding accommodation and also provided ongoing support. A significant number of these organisations had close links with black churches and religious affiliations.

The activism of black people in the field of social work has not been recognised in the social work profession. The history of social welfare and social work includes black men and women who founded various organisations to serve the needs of their communities. Many of these activists were guided by principles of self-help, race pride, solidarity and mutual aid, where community-defined aspirations become the focal priority at the grass roots level. In various ways, their social welfare activities were shaped by the needs of their communities.

Adam (1978) draws attention to the importance of community in the development of solidarity and resistance to oppression. In this context, community over time generates social networks and ways of surviving, understanding life experiences as modes of resistance. These experiences are set within realities defined by the group itself.

Conclusion

The African heritage in the development of social welfare provides the background and context in which the institution of enslavement influenced social welfare reform. The ideology of race entered the broad spectrum of social welfare during a critical period when the free flow of ideas from social reformers conceptualised and shaped state and charitable welfare instruments. The institution of enslavement produced paradigms of extreme human degradation which philanthropists and social reformers drew on in their efforts to ameliorate the deprivations of the English poor providing a baseline for social reforms. These areas of study promote greater understanding of the ways in which the cultural virus of racism continues to permeate social welfare institutions in modern Britain. The unfolding of 'hidden' histories of African-descended people and social welfare reveals a continuity of cultural helping processes that have sustained black people for generations in their efforts to improve their life conditions against all odds. The institution of enslavement inadvertently reinforced various helping processes, providing further impetus for African people to help one another. The active components of black helping processes were apparent in the lives of the enslaved and 'free' African community and translated into the affirmation of African cultural value systems amidst the ravages of enslavement, racism, poverty and destitution. These areas of study represent an important account of cultural forms that have become the focus of African-centred research in social welfare.

Chapter 4
Expanding the philosophical base of social work: African-centred worldviews

The unique feature of our culture is that its root and base is Africa. To acknowledge its origins is also to identify the unchanging seam, which is common to all Black cultures in the Diaspora. (Bryan *et al.*, 1985:183)

African-centred worldviews have emerged as an important cultural foundation source in the study of black people, their lived experiences, social practices, survival, wellbeing and understanding of the world. The articulation of these worldviews suggests that European and African worldviews have validity only under limiting conditions. However, this standpoint does not imply that only the philosophical traits of a particular worldview characterise people in that ethnic group; rather, this perspective implies that set of philosophical traits of a particular worldview is dominant (Dixon, 1976).

For many decades, black scholars and researchers have argued for an alternative social science paradigm that affirms the traditions, history and visions of African people (Akbar, 1985; Nobles, 1985; Asante, 1987; Schiele, 1994). Consequently, there is now a large body of academic literature that articulates African-centred epistemologies (for example, Scheurich and Young, 1997). This chapter maps the contours of African-centred worldviews as an interpretative framework for human behaviour and seeks to explore cultural elements as products for social theory and practice. In this section, I present an analysis of African-centred worldviews highlighting the problematics and critiques that have surrounded these sociocultural perspectives.

African-centred paradigms are based upon African-centred worldviews that reflect the social philosophies of ancient and traditional Africa to interpret a distinctive African school of thought. Many scholars have argued that in this way diverse human realities can be explored. Moreover, this approach contributes to our understanding of human existence without Eurocentric philosophical outlooks shaping a frame of reference as the context for analysis of black social realities (Nobles, 1985; Asante, 1987; Karenga, 1993).

African-centred discourse
African-centred worldviews rest upon the notion of a distinctive African philosophy that embraces various schools of thought which are derived from classical African civilisations as the baseline for conceptions of human beings

and the universe. Africa is viewed as the source of historical beginnings, templates of culture, belief systems, philosophies, values and knowledge of the world which all inform African cultural identities.

Over the past decades philosophers have articulated traditional and contemporary African social thought in both oral and written literatures as forms of philosophy that have brought into sharp focus the absence of persons of African and African descent in mainstream philosophical literature. For example, Keita (1994) proposes that African philosophical traditions can be divided into three distinct phases: classical, medieval and modern. Classical philosophical tradition is located in the classical ancient civilisations of Kemet, Axum (Ethopia) and Nubia. The ethical and cosmological writings of ancient Egypt and Nubians are to be considered philosophy. These are contained in *Coming Forth by Day* (The Book of the Dead). There is also a history of philosophical ideas enshrined within the civilisations of Axum articulated in the theological-metaphysical writings in the Ge'ez language (Diop, 1987;1991).

The second phase of African social thought relates to the periods when African states of Ghana, Mali and Songhay were in existence. Thirdly, modern philosophy embraces several trends in contemporary African social thought (Oruka, 1990). These trends represent the seat of long and protracted debates about the nature of African philosophy. I do not intend to enter into this debate at this juncture, however, this discussion of African philosophy 'simply suggests shared orientations born of similar cultural experiences' (Gyekye, 1987:x). This approach is based upon the 'underlying cultural unity or identity of the various individual thinkers that justifies references to varieties of thought as wholes, such as Western, European or [Chinese] philosophy' (Karenga, 1994:52).

In a similar vein, Diop (1987, 1991) explores the historical continuity of Africa in his identification of two layers of African history. The first layer is a general history of Africa that embraces antiquity including the totality of African peoples, and the second is African history consisting of the local histories of segments of African people dispersed by external forces, such as enslavement and colonialism. African philosophy, therefore, 'is a universal discourse or philosophy with diverse problematics and methods; peoples in various epochs contribute to the discourse; out of contributions from diverse traditions' (Bewaji, 1995:108).

The field of philosophy considers questions about the nature of human existence. Over time these questions have led philosophers to reflect upon the human experience in the search for answers to fundamental questions about life and the nature of humankind. These considerations have provided the basic underpinnings for the structure and ordering of philosophical principles to distil the essence of human beings. This reflective activity encapsulates the interplay of reason and sense experience in shaping epistemologies. Epistemologies, sources of knowledge, are intrinsically bound by historical period, culture and ideology: the questions we ask about the world and human behaviour reflect our life experiences, our culture and our historical development. Philosophical assumptions, then, underlie our ways of knowing.

In this context, black scholars have sought to articulate the voice of African and African-descended peoples in the reclamation of African character in various fields. These efforts are now framed by African-centred social thought. This project gives identity to a new field of discourse. In various ways, this discourse is conditioned by its European heritage in challenging its claims to truth, universal knowledge and value neutrality. Moreover, this understanding gives rise to the need to explore the worldviews and lived experiences of black people in the process of surviving and contemporaneously forging social change through community regeneration, and cultural and spiritual renewal that embraces human possibilities.

African-centred social thought has emerged as a critical, deconstructive and reconstructive project that challenges the definitive characterisation of what it is to be human within the context of Enlightenment philosophies. Moreover, this enterprise seeks to organise, study and analyse cultural data in the cultures and philosophies of African people under the umbrella of African philosophy. African-centred endeavours contend that there exists an emotional, cultural, intellectual and psychological connection between all African people wherever they are located. This project seeks to validate the experiences of African peoples as well as critique the exclusion and marginalisation of African knowledge systems from educational and mainstream scholarship. This intellectual exercise began with a decolonised study of Africa from African-centred perspectives. This concept of decolonisation refers to breaking with the ways in which the African human condition is defined and shaped by the dominant context and asserting an understanding of social realities informed by local experiences (hooks, 1984). This trend in African philosophy has its roots in Pan-African social thought and the civil rights movement in the USA it also spans the Caribbean, Europe, Africa and other areas of the diaspora in seeking to free African and African-descended peoples from racialised domination. In this context, the decolonisation of Africa and the Caribbean and the reclamation of indigenous cultures have strongly influenced this discourse.

There are various strands that have shaped and defined African-centred social thought and these include African socialism, Consciencism, scientific socialism and African humanism. These strands draw upon eminent black scholars and activists over the past 200 years who have been instrumental in defining an African-centred intellectual school of thought. Black scholars – notably Ani, Asante, Akbar, Nobles, Hillard, Diop, Obenga, T'Shaka, Blyden, Clarke and Karenga – have been engaged in the process of reclaiming ancient African philosophical systems to interpret a distinctive African school of thought. This project proposes that these ideals can assist in shaping futures for African peoples throughout the world. It is claimed that 'any meaningful and authentic study of peoples of African descent must begin and proceed with Africa as the centre, not periphery' (Abarry, 1990:123).

Liberation philosophies

In engaging in this discussion, I use the term liberation philosophy coined by English and Kalumba (1996:7). This term captures the ultimate concern of all anti-colonial, political and social thinkers and the term 'appears to be a timely, umbrella expression with respect to all African social, political and philosophical works for the foreseeable future'.

Nkombe and Smet (1978 cited in Outlaw, 1998) provide a useful survey of liberation philosophies and they identify three groupings. First, there are expositions of liberation philosophy that adhere to redressing the political, social and culture situation of African people under the conditions of colonialism, imperialism and racism. Second there is an explicit attempt to separate and analyse the present constraints of African societies while remaining true to African ideals. In addition, a recognition of the existence of philosophy in traditional Africa and seeks to 'examine its philosophical elements as found in its various manifestations, and systematically elaborate them as repositories of wisdom and esoteric knowledge' (Outlaw, 1990:234).

The third grouping is the critical school that engages in a deeply critical stance of Western/European conceptions of science and philosophy. These identified groupings do not capture the broader perspectives that not only deconstruct conventional paradigms which initiate and support the historical disparagement of African people, but seek to explore African ways of knowing and lived experiences as well. This school of thought is devoted to serving the interests of black peoples by examining their contribution to human society. This venture is not merely an intellectual exercise: it also makes important connections between theory and practice in its envelopment of systematic knowledge and social action.

Karenga (1993:19) interprets this project by advocating 'an investigative and applied discipline [that] poses the paradigm of theory and practice merging into active self-knowledge which leads to positive social change'. The civil rights and Pan-African movements articulated a vision that academia should be directed towards service to the community and 'dedicated not only to understanding self, society and the world but also to changing them in a positive developmental way in the interest of human history and advancement' (Karenga, 1988:32).

The liberation trend in African philosophy has proved the most intense and heated subject of debate, which continues to provoke controversial discussion within academic circles. This has arisen in part due to the growth of scholarship and literature in this area of study. The debates about whether African people have philosophies or can philosophise have given way to a broader range of concerns located within the understanding of intellectual practices and legacies of people of African descent within the diaspora.

The civil rights and black consciousness movements in the USA, the 'negritude' movement in France and its colonies and Pan-African movements in the Caribbean and Africa serve as sources for the reconstruction of intellectual histories (Outlaw, 1996). These developments have drawn upon Africa as providing the template and context for articulating the lived experiences of African people throughout the diaspora. This project involves the reclamation and restoration of African civilisation as a corrective to the historical disparagement of its people. In this way, it is claimed, the histories and philosophical insights of Africa can assist in the cultural and spiritual rebirth and renewal of people of African descent and contribute to the humanity of all peoples.

These orientations are embedded within the African-centred conceptual framework that has been developed by Asante (1980;1987;1990) in establishing the field of discourse. There have been various definitions and expressions of African-centred social thought. However, they all share a concern to present an alternative way of knowing the world. This intellectual exercise seeks to bring people of African descent from the margins of European social thought to the centre of postmodern history.

According to Asante (1990) the African-centred intellectual idea is distinguished by five characteristics:

- an intense interest in psychological location as determined by symbols, motifs, rituals and signs

- a commitment to finding the subject place of Africans in any social, political, economic or religious phenomenon with implications for questions of sex, gender and class

- a defence of African cultural elements as historically valid in the context of art, music and literature

- a celebration of 'centredness' and agency and a commitment to lexical refinement that eliminates pejoratives about Africans and other people

- a powerful imperative from historical sources to revise the collective text of African people

Asante (1980:5) suggests an African cultural system in which all African people participate, 'although it is modified according to specific histories and nations'. The grounding of African-centred thought is located in *Njia*, 'the collective expression of the Afrocentric worldview based in the historical experience of African people'. Thus, dispensing with the legacy of European Enlightenment representations of Africans in intellectual thought gives rise to new criticism that assists in 'a cultural reconstruction that incorporates the African perspective as a part of an entire human transformation' (1980:6). In this way, African people are given subject place with agency in the study of African phenomena. According to Asante (1980:7), one of the important aspects of this project is the reclamation of the African origins of ancient Egypt (Kemet) and the Nile Valley civilisations. Within this context, classical African civilisations can be 'points of reference for an African perspective in much the same way as Greece and Rome are in the European world'.

Asante (1980:34) maintains that furnished with this new information which will expand human perspectives on knowledge, transcultural analysis will become possible. Therefore, armed with this new information and emanating innovative methodologies, 'Africology will transform community and social sciences, as well as arts and humanities and assist in constructing a new, perhaps more engaging way to analyse and synthesise reality'.

African-centred theories propose that this is the most effective way of studying and understanding African people and their communities. This approach suggests an orientation in approaching and interpreting data. Thus African-centred theory may be viewed as mapping the boundaries and contours of this disciplinary field.

Before I discuss the problematics that have fuelled the intense and heated debates concerning African-centred theories, I want to sketch the primary principles and values that make up this normative construct (Akbar, 1976; Asante, 1987; L. Myers, 1988; Asante, 1990; Schiele, 1997, 2000; Graham, 1999, 2000).

African-centred worldviews begin with a holistic conception of the human condition which spans the cosmological (an aspect of philosophy that considers the nature and structure of the universe), ontological (the essence of all things), and axiological (an area of philosophy that considers the nature of values and value preferences in a culture).

African-centred philosophy is a holistic system based upon values and ways of living which are reinforced through rituals, music, dance, story-telling, proverbs, metaphors and the promoting of family; rites of passage, naming ceremonies, child-rearing, birth, death, elderhood and values of governance. The principles and values that underpin the African-centred worldview (Akbar, 1976; Asante, 1987; L. Myers, 1988; Asante, 1990; Schiele, 1997) are:

- the interconnectedness of all things
- the spiritual nature of human beings
- collective/individual identity and the collective/inclusive nature of family structure
- oneness of mind, body and spirit
- the value of interpersonal relationships

African-centred worldviews
The interconnectedness of all things
Within the cosmological perspective of the African-centred worldviews, all elements of the universe – people, animals and inanimate objects – are viewed as interconnected. Since they are dependent upon each other, they are, in essence, considered as one (Mbiti, 1970; Nobles, 1985). Human reality is unified and we divide unity into parts only because of the limitations of our

present knowledge. Asante (1990) expresses unification through a statement credited to the Zulu peoples: 'I am river, I am mountain, I am tree, I am love, I am emotion, I am beauty, I am lake, I am cloud, I am sun, I am sky, I am mind, I am one with one.'

For Akbar (1976:176), the unity of 'the African cosmos is like a spider web; its least element cannot be touched without making the whole vibrate. Everything is connected, interdependent.' These relationships provide individuals with a sense of purpose and connection with families and community. This is because the self 'cannot be complete if it remains enclosed, but it has to seek out the other if it is to become actualised...a person can only be a human when other people are there to complete his or her humaness. The individual cannot be human alone' (Holdstock, 2000:105). Moreover, the maintenance of harmonious social relationships supports the development of positive self-esteem and social competence. Social problems and human dysfunction arise when people become alienated and disconnected from their interdependent human relationships.

The interconnectedness of all things sees no separation between the material and the spiritual 'reality is at one and inseparably spiritual and material' (L. Myers, 1988:24) as all reality (universe) begins from a single principle. Human beings are perceived as an integral part of nature, and living in harmony with the environment helps them to become one with all reality. The concept of oneness relates to those not yet born and those who have died: all human beings are linked spiritually across time and space. As Schiele (1994:18) declares, 'the focus on interconnectedness recognises that people are spiritual (i.e., nonmaterial) beings who are connected with each other through the spirit of the Creator'. The spiritual aspect of human beings transcends the spheres of time and space.

The interconnectedness of human beings spiritually is translated socially, so that the human being is never an isolated individual but always the person in the community. The community defines the person, as Mbiti, (1970:141) explains: 'I am because we are; and because we are, therefore I am.' Holdstock (2000:105) captures the essence of this concept when he uses the Zulu expression, '*umuntu ngumuntu ngabantu*', which means that a person is a person through other persons. Self-knowledge is rooted in 'being centred in one's self, one's own experience, one's history' (Verharen, 1995:65). To become aware of the cultural self is an important process that connects a person spiritually to others within a culture. It is the universal network of energies that generates sustenance for individuals and communities and, in so doing, self-knowledge within the context of one's cultural base and connection with others provides the basis for transformation, spiritual development and wellbeing.

The spiritual nature of human beings
    Spirituality forms the cornerstone of African-centred worldviews and is the essence of human beings. Spirituality has been defined as 'that invisible substance that connects all human beings to each other and to a creator' (Schiele, 1994:18). The spiritual essence of human beings requires a shift in thinking towards valuing human beings above the social and economic status which has been assigned to them. For example, who you are, your personhood, comes about through your relationship with the community. As Karenga (1997) proposes, personhood evolves through the process of becoming and this negates the idea that personhood is achieved simply by existence. The process of being is marked by successive stages of integration or incorporation into the community. Life is a series of passages: a process whereby a person is accorded the challenge to grow, change and develop to attain moral, intellectual and social virtues within the context of community.

Collective/individual identity and collective/inclusive nature of the twinlineal family structure
    The individual cannot be understood separately from other people (L. Myers, 1988). The collective nature of identity is expressed in the African proverb 'I am because we are and because we are therefore I am' (Mbiti, 1970:141). These philosophical assumptions transmit to the psyche a sense of belonging to the collective and of being part of the whole. This is because mutuality and individuality are inextricably linked in the concept of self. The individual's moral growth and development facilitates the growth of others (Holdstock, 2000).

    From these assumptions of collective identity follows the emphasis upon human similarities or commonalities rather than upon individual differences. The collective nature of human beings entails collective responsibility for what happens to individuals. 'Whatever happens to the individual happens to the whole group and whatever happens to the whole group happens to the individual' (Mbiti, 1970:141). The collective identity of human beings links the conception of the family to its structures and functioning. Twinlineal is a term used for black families, refering to the fact that African family lineages come from both the mother and father rather than *only* the mother or father as in matrilineal and patrilineal family systems. The family structure also includes

71

members who are not biologically related and an extensive network of cousins (T'Shaka, 1995). This has immediate implications for social work: 'social workers have found themselves utterly confused when they have attempted to list, define or describe black families utilising the guidelines which have grown from their own experiences' (Akbar, 1976:180).

The notion of half-siblings prevalent within social work theory and practice, for example, is incomprehensible; it does not exist within an African-centred worldview. Ryan and Walker (1993) discuss the increase in family breakdowns:

> *some of these relationships eventually end too. As the years progress, there may be a tangled network of **full siblings, half-siblings and stepsiblings**. It should be remembered that these family networks are neither abnormal nor unusual and it is important for children to understand this.* (T. Ryan and Walker, 1993:28, emphasis added)

Ryan and Walker go on to describe a family network as follows:

> *Pete and Mary married in May 1980. Pete became Wayne's stepfather, Pete and Mary had two children, Lisa and Alan. Mary told Wayne that Lisa and Alan were his 'half' brother and sister. Annie and Cheryl were Lisa and Alan's half-sisters and Wayne's stepsisters.* (1993:28)

The model is then illustrated to indicate complicated family ties, showing circles that overlap each other to help a child understand how the family network developed.

The underlying precept of 'half-sibling' becomes a value-based supposition within social work practice that is manifested where contact arrangements with 'half-siblings' may be viewed as less important than those with 'full siblings'. In my experience, and that of many other professionals working in the field of child-care, neither these concepts nor these assumptions reflect the realities of black children. Thus the ethnocentric worldview constructs a 'universalism' of social work practice and imposes a value system and construct which may compromise the psychological wellbeing of black children.

For the same reason, the therapeutic tool of the ecomap does not capture the realities of some black families or of the network of cousins and other family members beyond the 'extended family'. This more complex picture, of families which include members who are not biologically related, is reflected in developing African-centred designs for social work practice where there is an emphasis on being part of a group, spiritually as well as physically, as an essential ingredient of identity. The failure of the social work profession to comprehend this critical proposition is one of the reasons why black professionals and the black community were so vociferously opposed to the one-way traffic of transracial placements. The children were considered a loss to the whole community, not just physically but as a loss felt spiritually by the collective – the whole community – worldwide.

African-centred worldviews regard children as the collective responsibility of communities. The African proverb, 'It takes a village to raise a child', expresses the view that child-rearing is a collective responsibility, rather than a concern for individual nuclear families. Children are highly valued in general, as 'of the community', and they therefore cannot be deemed illegitimate (Suda, 1997).

Oneness of mind, body and spirit and the value of interpersonal relationships

There is no division between mind, body and spirit in African-centred paradigms. They are each given equal value and are believed to be interrelated (Mbiti, 1970). The development and knowledge of self, mind, body and spirit are the hallmark of human objectives to seek divinity through *Maat* (truth, justice, righteousness, harmony, balance, order, propriety, compassion and reciprocity) within the self and through reaching a state of optimal health (Chissell, 1994). To promote personhood, optimal health requires optimal emotional health, physical health, intellectual health and spiritual health. These principles underlie the need to achieve harmony with the forces of life. King (1994:20) outlines the process of achieving a harmonious way of living. He suggests the combination of co-operating with natural forces that influence events and experiences while at the same time 'taking responsibility for one's life by consciously choosing and negotiating the direction and paths one will follow'.

African-centred worldviews include the concept of balance. The task of all living things is to maintain balance in the face of adverse external forces. When this inner peace is compromised, the psychological, social and physical wellbeing of a person is threatened.

Using these values and principles as a guide, Karenga (1993) has developed a theory of cultural and social change. The Kwaida theory proposes that examples of alienation, degradation, self-hatred and dysfunction within black communities may be directly related to a misplaced consciousness. Karenga (1993) contends that this is symptomatic of a cultural crisis that faces communities in European/Western contexts where marginalisation and institutional racism are an integral part of societies. The philosophy of Kwaida is expressed as an orientation towards corrective action that includes the reconstruction of cultural values on the basis of a critical reading of African cultural antecedents. Thus Kwaida is a prescriptive theory of cultural and social change located in seven basic areas of cultural and social life. These correctives are advanced in the areas of religion, history, social, economic and political organisations, creativity and ethos (Karenga, 1993).

The core of the Kwaida theory advances seven principles, the *Nguzo Saba*, to provide a guide to cultural and social change and the organisation of black life. These include *Umoja* (unity), *Kujichagulia* (self-determination), *Ujima* (collective work and responsibility), *Ujamaa* (co-operative economics), *Nia* (purpose), *Kuumba* (creativity) and *Imani* (faith).See Table 5.1 for more information

Expanding ethical frameworks of social work

There has been growing interest in the ethical dimensions of social work and the various ways in which organising principles direct decision-making and the professional behaviour of social workers. Ethics have been at the heart of social work since its inception. Throughout its history the profession has embraced concerns about what is just and unjust as an ongoing consideration that gives meaning to its mission (Reamer, 1993).

In contrast to other helping professions, the central place of ethics in social work highlights its anchorage to normative organising principles. This approach is conceptualised in the use of the rules and guidelines found in CCETSW's *Rules and Regulations for social work students*, the British Association of Social Workers *Code of Ethics* and the National Association of Social Workers *Code of Ethics*. Many commentators are sceptical about the value of codes of ethics because they are surrounded by problematics that limit their use as a guide in social work practice. Banks (1995) believes a code of ethics is useful in maintaining a professional identity but warns that such codes have become increasingly irrelevant in the context of changes in the management and delivery of social services. On the other hand, Reamer (1997:342) argues that a code of ethics 'can serve a terribly valuable service to the extent that they cite the issues and concepts that practitioners ought to factor into their thinking and decisions'. Moreover, the growth in ethical concerns has generated a body of knowledge in relation to ethical dilemmas and decision-making to enable social workers to deal with complex ethical issues as they arise in a competent manner.

Reamer (1998), writing about the history of social work, draws attention to the shift away from the preoccupation with the morality of the client towards moral reasoning and the ethics of practitioners in the pursuit of managing risk behaviour. This shift in focus suggests that the code of ethics espoused by the profession is related to, and driven by, contemporary issues within the context of social, political and economic contingencies.

The importance of values in social work has given rise to an abundance of literature articulating core values and engaging in discussions about the nature and conflict of values, and ethical dilemmas that arise in practice which affect social workers' decision-making and social actions (i.e. Biestek, 1961; Reamer, 1993, 1995; Banks, 1995).

Values commonly referred to in the literature are individual worth and dignity, respect for persons, client self-determination, social justice, empowerment, equal opportunity, commitment to social change and confidentiality. These values and principles are viewed as a primary guide to effective social work practice. The increasing complexity of social work in modern society has brought to the fore new sets of ethical concerns and dilemmas, in part due to the changes in provision to meet social needs and technological advances.

For example, in recent years social work in Britain has become an occupation characterised by compliance with regulations, procedures and assessments. As a consequence, the social and political context in which social work interventions take place has become partially dissolved. The regulated role of social workers is located in the changes in social work education where, as C. Jones (1996:191) observes: 'there is no comparable system of social work education in the world which is so nationally uniform, uninspired, and tailored so closely to the requirements of state employers'. The narrow scope of social work education, embedded as it is in an emphasis upon a competency-led development of knowledge and skills:

> *assumes that competence is the sum of achieved competencies; it lacks the reflective knowledge and understanding which are different from separate skills; it discourages the innovation and creativity necessary to handle unforeseen problems; it reduces ethical and philosophical debate to simplistic and one-dimensional 'values'.* (Humphries, 1997: 650)

So far this discussion has focused upon social work ethics and values arising from a foundation of knowledge that is embedded within Western philosophical assumptions and social thought. In this way social work has adopted its heritage and therefore constitutes a mode of its expression (C. Clark, 2000).

In this sense, values inform belief systems and, as Webb and McBeath (1989:501) maintain:

> *ethical and moral theories are inscribed within particular periods of history, and are instrumental in maintaining political interests...which set standards and norms by which people should live and also promote modes of domination and forms of legitimation for professional bodies such as social work.*

As a consequence of this process, discussions about ethics and values are often presented within unproblematic frameworks incorporating ethical considerations that are held to be universally true. For example, definitions of self-determination, one of the pre-eminent values of social work, are located in an individualist Eurocentric value system. By contrast, African-centred social work recognises that self-determination has meanings in other ways that are inextricably linked to a collective as well as individual sense of identity and being (Graham, 1999). More specifically, as Dei (1999b:19) holds, 'understanding self as a "whole person" means the self multiplicated and yet connected to the collective. The self is a spiritual, emotional, cultural and psychological being, as well as a physical and material embodiment.' Thus, as Ewalt and Mokuau (1995) argue, group wellbeing is also part of self-determination. This is because subjugated groups and communities often seek to share their experiences, histories and cultures, and through these instruments develop group affinities. Independent action and thinking emerge from one's personhood, but are grounded in a shared sense of belonging (Dei, 1999a). In this way, black people may seek to 'strengthen connections with the group' and through this process they exercise intellectual agency in making choices about their lives.

These understandings call for critical thinking and reflection because the process of decision-making in social work is inextricably linked to personal and societal values. Critical thinking then becomes an important instrument in knowledge building for social work and demands that the contours of frameworks themselves be interrogated. Models of social work, such as African-centred approaches, demand critical examination about the definitions and boundaries of frameworks themselves as well as considerations within them. In so doing, questions can be raised and lines of inquiry pursued as valuable and important routes to knowledge (Gambrill, 1997).

According to Rhodes (1992:40) ethics are 'the study of how to live, of how to achieve human excellence, which in turn encompasses everything in our lives, from our daily personal activities to our professional behaviour as social workers' (cited in Manning, 1997:224).

Ethics in social work are concerned with doing right and taking a course of action that is morally necessary given the circumstances of given situations. Social work as a profession has a moral function over and above individual morality and its ethical issues located in practice. Social actions and decisions made by social workers are related to what social workers value and indirectly to society's priorities and value preferences. Social work conveys a moral function about what is right or good in a culture (Manning, 1997). It has been argued that social work has a moral duty to 'make the invisible visible' and examine beyond the surface of dominant ideologies to ascertain patterns of oppression hidden and conveyed in professional language and behaviour. This approach provides the opportunity to promote the purpose of social work in directing ethical actions.

Challenging dominant forms of knowledge in social work

Some critiques maintain that Western forms of knowledge in shaping and defining frameworks of social work are too diverse to permit broad generalisations. However, many black commentators and feminists call attention to oppressive thought structures and dominant cultural and social norms that inform theoretical models for practice across the helping professions including social work (Dominelli and McLeod, 1989; Burman, 1994; Schiele, 2000). For example, commentators have identified one of the predominant features of Western society as being the central place of the individual, and this purview guides views of reality in shaping knowledge of human development and behaviour (Clough,1960; Gordon, 1975; Akbar, 1984; Schiele, 2000). The individual took pride of place in early social work theory and practice and continues take a central position across the field of social work theory and practice.

Under these circumstances, Friedlander (1976:1) holds that in reality social work values are far from being presented as unproblematic, he writes, 'the basic values of social work do not spring up like wild flowers by the way side; they are instead rooted in the deep and subtle beliefs that nourish civilisation'. Therefore, it is within this context that the opportunity to explore and integrate knowledge systems from different domains becomes apparent.

Social work commentators have given limited attention to knowledge systems of subjugated groups as a source of ethical theory building. The neglect and marginalisation of this rich source of human knowledge can be viewed as a lost opportunity to explore new directions for social work and reaffirm the profession's dedication to confronting issues of oppression and discrimination. Moreover, the advancement of the social work profession demands an expansion of its ethical foundation to give voice to a global understanding of human moral development.

Maat as a source of ethical theory building

The ethical system of *Maat* has been the locus of considerable scholarly work among black commentators over the past decades. The concept of *Maat* is fundamental to Kemetic (Ancient Egyptian) ethics and thus underpins African-centred worldviews. Black scholars, such as Karenga (1994) have analysed the ethical framework of *Maat* in an attempt to discover and revitalise core conceptions of the *Maatian* ideal. The concepts of *Maat* are translated into the language of modern moral discourse in order to uncover cultural connections with an ancestral past. In this context, ancient values can assist in the quest for community regeneration, revitalisation and cultural renewal in creating new visions and futures. Furthermore, *Maat* has within its meanings an elasticity that allows for 'creative thought about new and ongoing challenges to the African and human community', and it can therefore, be a useful paradigm to the world (Karenga, 1994:557). These important insights regarding *Maatian* ethics reveal its congruence as an important source for theory building in social work. Unlike customary conceptualisation of spirituality and social work and its linkages with theology, *Maatian* ethics respect and embrace the divine but do not engage in theological debates and have no all-embracing laws (Karenga, 1994). In this way, holistic and ecological approaches to helping invite spiritual dimensions that are often missed or neglected in social work.

Maat represents the principle upon which society and the cosmos are based and a moral and ethical guide to life. Frankfort (1948:6) describes *Maat* as a 'divine order established at the time of creation and it is manifest in nature as the normalcy of phenomena ... in society as justice and ... in an individual's life as truth'.

Obenga (1990) articulates the complexity of the *Maatian* ideal expressed in four domains of human life: (1) its universality and representations of harmony and place; (2) justice is at the centre of social formations and practice; (3) emphasis upon duty in the context of community; (4) personhood through concretising universal order in oneself. The principle of *Maat*, then, encapsulates a multiplicity of meanings that include the virtues of truth, justice, propriety, harmony, balance, reciprocity and order. These virtues represent the keys to human perfectability.

The core concept of *Maat* is rightness in nature and righteousness (justice). *Maat* is a spiritual knowledge system and method of organising relationships with others and the world. Reciprocity is central to the expression of *Maat* and has a pivotal place in various forms of social welfare in communities throughout the world. The parameters of social welfare discourse are largely confined to post-industrial societies where the professionalisation of the art of helping replaced family indigenous systems of helping, reciprocity, sharing and redistribution (Jordan, 1997). As Karenga (1990b:361) observes, 'social welfare is a fundamental and continuing component of Maat'. In this context, Karenga (1990b) considers three forms of reciprocity expressed as *Maat*.

1. The compensatory reciprocity that refers to doing good is in turn rewarded by good.

2. The obligatory nature of reciprocity is based upon demands of justice. Therefore, 'do not replace good with evil and put not one thing in the place of another' (1990b:362).

3. When *Maat* is expressed as reciprocity, the doer cultivates *Maat* in others by example. Thus, reciprocity contributes to an expanding good in which all may flourish and the development of a moral community. In other words, 'it is not simply doing to others what you would expect, but acting in such a way you cultivate the context for the highest level of moral community and exchange' (1990b:368).

It is through reciprocity that expression of *Maat* is made real in personal and social practice. Therefore, in *Maat* both ideals and action are an ongoing activity and moral principles are expressed in the communal act of exchange.

The social concerns of Maatian ethics are cited in the quality of human relationships and the development of character. Human beings have a propensity towards goodness because the central place of spirituality considers the transformation potential of human beings to be vast and unlimited. Thus self-realisation takes place within a social context based upon the assumption that self-actualisation of humans is best achieved in morally grounded relations with others (Karenga, 1990b). Therefore, the individual is always a person rooted within the community where patterns of development are shaped in critical thought and social practice so that the collective and personal exist within a social context of reciprocal unity (Karenga, 1990b). These unifying principles encompass a diffusion of *Maat* across space and time, harmonising humans living, departed and yet to be born.

The principle of self-realisation is expressed within the ethics of care and responsibility where service to others is not only beneficial to others but also to oneself. Reciprocity between the community and the person is an investment in each other's happiness, wellbeing and development. This approach exemplifies the person in community where, through this spiritual transaction with other people, 'the individual become[s] conscious of his own being, his own duties, his privileges and responsibilities toward himself and towards other people' (Mbiti, 1970:141). These considerations are encapsulated in the words 'I think therefore we are.' The emphasis upon social practices located within *Maat* brings moral and ethical concerns to the heart of everyday life. This is because *Maat* represents principles of living rather than a static abstract concept of the mind. Therefore, one must do *Maat*: that is speak truth, do justice and walk each day in the path of rightness. *Maat,* then is a personal and social task: 'a lived concreteness which develops the Maatian person in context and process of building and sustaining a Maatian society' (Karenga, 1990a:33).

In other words, the aim is to live in harmony with nature and the ordered whole. This sense of unity between self and cosmos is highly revered in traditional Africa and reveals no split between material and spiritual aspects of knowing the world. Thus, according to Asante (1990:83) 'there is no difference between human beings in knowledge-of-themselves and the cosmos-being'. The maxim 'know thy self' referred to by Asante (1990) considers 'uncovering the inner ear' as the pinnacle of self-knowledge which evokes experiences of internal harmony. L. Myers (1988) maintains that wisdom based upon self-knowledge was located in symbolic imagery and rhythm. African realities embrace the union of opposites, the visible and invisible shaping and defining interpersonal relationships.

The path of *Maat* takes a spiral form or is a concentric circle that mimics the spiral motion of the cosmos, and justice followed the same path. The path of *Maat* correlated with human life on earth that goes through the same zig-zag pattern encapsulated in the words 'as above, so below' (T'Shaka, 1995). These contingencies translate into social life where individuals progress through the development of human character from a lower to a higher level through the cycles of life, as lessons of *Maat* and the cosmos are learnt. These lessons are internalised as thoughts and behaviour and transformed, rising to a perfection that realises the divine within. The process of growth and development represents the true meaning and joy of life.

The sacredness of womanhood in traditional African societies is exemplified in spiritual knowledge of the world and organisation of life. These tenets were told in metaphors of nature, cosmos and the spiritual connections of humans 'in the scheme of all that is spirit and in balance' (Warfield-Coppock, 1997:124).

Allen (1992) contends that devaluation of womanhood in contemporary societies is inextricably linked to the devaluation of woman-centred traditions and the spiritual life. In the spiritual realm the power of womanhood was central to spiritual knowledge, informing the basis of moral and ethical concerns. Gilligan (1988) suggests that women and men have distinctive moral outlooks. Women's moral understandings have been subjugated and excluded in conventional moral and ethical discourse. Gilligan (1988) contends that masculine thinking has taken precedence in philosophical discourse, thereby reaffirming patriarchal structures and patterns in society. According to Gilligan (1988) the ethical and moral orientations of both sexes are necessary for the moral conduct of society. From this perspective, woman-centredness as an organising principle in spiritual knowledge directs balance to mediate dominance and embrace female principles in social relationships. Thus the place and position of womanhood was assured. Woman-centred spiritual knowledge systems are not the exclusive preserve of ancient and traditional African societies but are found largely in the traditions of societies outside Western contexts.

The central concern of *Maat* in caring and compassion indicate the primary place of feminine principles in its meanings. *Maat* is expressed in the symbol of a female diety. Karenga (1994) proposes *Maat* as the personification of the mothering ideal. Moreover, as Dove (2000) observes, 'her presence and manifestation in institutional organisation and human culture ensured the righteous existence of humanity as part of the cosmos'. Doing *Maat* encapsulates the nature of caring enshrined in moral practices of mothering. These moral practices were expressed in compassion and caring for others and, in this way *Maat* flourished in the world. *Maat* creates an environment conducive to moral growth, culture and community (Karenga, 1994). *Maat* as a spiritual knowledge system emphasises mothering as a critical social skill that holds important cultural values.

Dove (2000) considers *Maat* (as the practice of mothering) to be a central tenet grounded in the veneration of womanhood. Mothering qualities are desirable attributes in society so that all human beings want to acquire these qualities. The term mothering embraces its proclivity towards mothering qualities, including caring and compassion for all human beings, which holds no emphasis upon gender. This is because one of the tenets of *Maat* is harmony, which is located in relationships of reciprocity.

Dove (2000) puts forth a conceptual framework of the Mother Centred Matrix that calls for a rethinking of matriarchal concepts that have characterised major discourses of traditional African societies. Her thesis draws attention to the principles of *Maat* expressed in both female and male governance. Both matriarchal and patriarchal orientations lay claim to dominance of either sex and thus can be are viewed as oppositional to *Maat*. A mother-centred matrix places *Maat* at the centre of ethical and moral systems and brings complementarity to the nature of male and female relationships because the spiritual orientation of society is based upon the sacred power of womanhood and life-affirming principles. Woman-centred spiritual systems help to maintain balance in social relationships because you cannot have justice and propriety without balance. The importance of mothering brings harmony and balance and ensures male governance displays feminine qualities and deference to feminine divinity. These conceptual tools give ethical reflection in the 'collective values, consideration of humanity and nature, ancestral esteem, love and respect for the family' and all members of the family practised the mothering ideal of *Maat*. These ethical considerations are expressed in the high value placed upon children and their upbringing. The child has an important and honourable place in African societies because the child creates a link between generations and ensures the continuation of life. The young and old are closest to the spiritual world and therefore have a special link expressed in communal relationships. Traditionally, elders took a major role in the education and socialisation of young children, affirming the adage 'wisdom embraces knowledge'. They provided the linchpin for generations comprised of adults, children and ancestors to secure the forward flow of community life (Wilcox, 1998).

Diallo and Hall (1989:44) consider the features of elderhood that contributed to the maintenance and forward flow of community:

Grandparents form the circle of elders. They represent the world of knowledge and constitute the supreme council of the village. To avoid the anger of the ancestors, with whom they can communicate through rituals and divination, they are supposed to know all the prohibitions and how to remedy any violations of a social taboo. They are wise and move thoughtfully. They are walking books of know how.

In this way, elders have a pivotal place in black communities to give children a sense of history, to teach and counsel, and to explain the path of life and its meanings. Fu-Kiau and Lukondo-Wamba (1988) bring to the fore the importance of child-care located within the context of community. They contend that in Western contexts babysitting is regarded as an insignificant activity and this task is usually given to inexperienced teenagers with nothing to do. Yet in many African societies, *Kindezi* (the term used to describe the task of caring) is 'the greatest honour that can be bestowed upon a person in Afrikan society'. According to Fu-Kiau and Lukondo-Wamba (1988:4), babysitting (child-care) is an ancient art taught to male and females that brings to the fore the 'wonderful skill of being responsible for another life and how to become a new living pattern' through which cultural values are transmitted from generation to generation. Looking after a child involves the art of caring and touching in shaping humankind and the future of its world environment. Young people are taught the art of caring through the supervision of an elder. Fu-Kiau and Lukondo-Wamba (1988) consider that *Kindezi* has freed the hands of African mothers so that they can participate in economic, political and social life in their communities. The practical skills of caring are described as an art and given a high status which creates a truly child-centred environment as expressed in the adage 'It takes a village to raise a child.'

Social work and spirituality

The place of spirituality in African-centred worldviews indicates that there is no distinction between the sacred and the secular. These considerations bring into sharp focus the scant regard for spirituality in social work. As Martin and Martin (1995:12) observe, 'professional social work could have been humanised, spiritualised and radicalised by black helping traditions ... making black people view it less as an instrument of social control and containment and more as a potent force for social change'.

Schiele (2000) discusses spirituality as the basis of African-centred social work in attempting to solve problems associated with oppression and spiritual alienation. He argues that existing models of social work place emphasis upon an epistemology that reflects a materialist view of reality. Ways of knowing are based upon the five senses, which de-emphasise the metaphysical impact on human behaviour and functioning. This perspective supports a proclivity towards self-worth based upon external criteria (material objects, prestige and status concerns, looks and so on) that become more important than concerns about the quality of interpersonal relationships and the collective wellbeing of people (L. Myers, 1988; Schiele, 1990).

L. Myers (1988) considers that this worldview has a tendency towards suboptimal thinking where fragmentation and segmentation characterise realities including people and genders. This fragmented view promotes difference to justify the exclusion and oppression of people. Optimal thinking, on the other hand, is derived from a worldview that promotes holistic thinking and spiritual development. The key values of life, self-worth and happiness are gained from within rather than from an emphasis upon external materialism. In addition, there is an emphasis upon how opposites are complementary and differences are independent rather than in conflict. This expanded notion of human possibilities gives voice to conventional ethical frameworks as a resource of enrichment. Moreover, the space to articulate spirituality comes at an appropriate time when the profession is reviewing its own use of spirituality in practice (Walz and Ritchie, 2000). Until recently, there has been limited discussion and literature about social work and spirituality.

There are many and varied definitions of spirituality. Canda (1988:43) sees spirituality as

> *concerned with the distinctively spiritual aspect of human experience as it is interwoven with all other aspects. The spiritual aspect refers to experience of a quality of sacredness and meaningfulness in self, other people, the non human world, and the ground of being.*

Okundaye *et al.* (1999:372) provide a similar view of spirituality as 'the wholeness of what it is to be human'. The concepts surrounding the term 'spirituality' have been strongly linked with religion. Indeed, social work's origins can be found in Judeo-Christian religious traditions. Canda (1988) discusses the history of social work and the process of secularisation that replaced Christian social work traditions. Although several authors have called for a return to religious as well as spiritual concerns in social work, the possibility of sectarian bias has dampened professional interest generally in reviving these links between religion and social work. In recent discussions about spirituality it is argued that spirituality is not necessarily based upon religious affiliations. People may choose to express their spirituality in various ways devoid of religious considerations.

The spiritual dimension of life is often a neglected area, both in social work practice and in the field of social work generally. Human beings, when confronted with life difficulties and perhaps experiencing pain and suffering find questions about the meaning of life often come to the fore. Human beings are essentially social beings, and for many people purpose gives meaning in their lives. For many people purpose and meaning is located in their communities as this is where meaning and purpose evolve with reference to, and in encounters with, others (Wells Irme, 1984).

Safoa, The National African and Caribbean Mental Health Network, agrees with this view and calls for services to 'reflect a view of the individual as part of a community living in physical, psychological, social and spiritual worlds'. In this way, spiritual values can give meaning to life experiences and insights into the possibilities inherent within the helping process. Spiritual principles can assist in seeking resolutions to trials and tribulations inherent within the human condition. Canda (1988) calls for a spiritually sensitive helping relationship that embraces empathy, caring, respect and compassion.

Bullis (1996) argues that there is a need to consider spirituality in social work and offers the following rationale. Traditionally, the profession of social work has been strongly influenced by spiritual concerns. Indeed, its origins are deeply embedded within spirituality and religion. Despite the absence of spirituality in social work texts, the spiritual dimension of life experience continues to be an important element of social work practice.

In addition, social work and spirituality are closely linked in promoting common interests and self- respect. Spirituality embraces personal and social healing that is in line with helping processes in social work. Moreover, spirituality is dedicated to process and can assist social work models of inter- vention to function more effectively in modern society. In this way, spirituality and social work can learn from each other in promoting personal and social transformation.

Finally, spiritual knowledge can assist social workers to know and under- stand spiritual dimensions of a person's worldview in devising helping strategies within assessment processes.

African-centred worldviews – critiques and problematics

Critical reviews of Afrocentricity have focused upon various problematics that emerge from this discipline. Some of these discussions are located within what constitutes the definition of the term 'African'. Definitions of the term

'African' invite the complicated meanings invested in the term following Europe's historical encounters with Africa. The task of defining 'African' is a controversial and difficult one. African identities are not limitless but do not mesh neatly into an overall fixed entity. Asante (1990:9), for example, takes the following approach: 'by African, I mean clearly a "composite African" not a specific discrete African orientation which would rather mean ethnic identification'. Asante (1990) quite clearly rejects biological determinism and maintains that the Afrocentric project is not based upon skin colour or biology and should not be confused with these biological theories. At the same time, he argues that it is a fallacy to assume that all African people are African-centred. The word African-centred is not a race-defining label but refers to a worldview and is principally an approach to data. It is knowledge that emerges from various treatments of data and that provides a framework for discursive practices within the field of study. For example, there are African-centred orientations in the important and standard works of European scholars such as Davidson, Bernal, Massey, Herskovits and Lubicz.

This perspective views phenomena from the standpoint of the African person as subject rather than object. The process of locating African people as the subject rests upon a critique of conventional notions of European Enlightenment social thought that has excluded the 'other' as a major source of explanations for social, philosophical and political life. In this way, the limits of social and political thought have shifted to create new arenas for study. African-centred theories embrace an intrinsic desire to document the socio-historical and cultural realities of people of African descent. In this critical context the repositioning of African people takes place and this location generates new analytical content, focus and orientation. This expanded definition of social life is validated and interrogated.

Karenga (1993) argues that African-centredness does not impute anything more to the conceptual category than is indicated in the terms European, Asian or Chinese. The discussion of this approach is important because many commentators have disparaged consideration of Africa's intellectual heritage. Zahan (1970:3) captures this scenario when he writes:

> *As strange as it may seem, no one in the West is astonished at the nuances and subtleties of Japanese or Chinese thought; but let an investigator document certain African ideas and he is considered a rash if not completely reckless 'interpreter'. It is almost as if the refinement of the mind were the heritage of one part of mankind and not another, unless one wants to assert by this strange value judgement*

that thought and reflection are necessarily expressed by a single category of signifiers. (quoted in Keita, 1994:208)

Thus, the underlying cultural unity of Africa accounts for the references to varieties of thought as wholes in a similar vein as Western European thought.

The emancipatory strand of African philosophy is closely associated with notions of commonalities and shared orientations among people of African descent that are strong enough to create a worldview in spite of the wide variations of experiences and geographical location. These commonalities arise from a shared experience of enslavement, colonialisation, struggles, and psychological and spiritual collectivity that produce arenas of similarity or connection.

This discussion draws attention to two important questions. First, in what ways are those identified as African or African-descended peoples orientated towards African-centred themes given that, according to Outlaw (1997:127), people of African descent 'share important aspects of their being with peoples of European descent'? African-centred social thought contends that although African people throughout the diaspora undoubtedly do share important aspects of their being with European peoples, the prevailing emphasis upon this aspect of their being negates and suppresses their African heritage which continues to inform their social realities and everyday living. As I have argued elsewhere, the dominant social and political orientation of cultural assimilation in European societies continues to suppress African identities as outmoded and not in keeping with the so-called modern age. However, many people of African descent view Africa as a homeland in symbolic, metaphysical and cosmological terms. In this regard, it is important to appreciate shifting African identities throughout the diaspora and the place of African cultural social forms and practices in the realities of everyday lives.

The development of culturally informed personal and social identities is important to the wellbeing of individuals and communities in maintaining cultural integrity and self-determining social practices.

Foucault's (1980) discourse analysis is helpful in deconstructing text to reveal the politics hidden in theories and methods as the configurations of knowledge become the subject of inquiry. These techniques of deconstruction have revealed the dynamics of domination and power relations in conventional knowledge. In this way, ascribed social and personal identities ('the ones the dominant culture has taught them to despise') have been used to dislodge power relations and open up space and opportunities for the development of subjectivities and to promote social change (Young,

1990:166). Afrocentricity offers the intellectual expansion of the continuing history-making struggles of African and African-descended peoples.

This discussion raises important questions concerning the presuppositions located in ideas that suggest a totalising discourse: for example, that all African people through shared lines of ancestry share forms of subjectivity or orientation that are closely associated to a geographical site of origin. In this way, several black scholars have been criticised for conflating ideas of cultural unity to support political and social agendas. Similar criticisms have been levelled against women's studies as falsely generalising the similarities of women. In this way, womanhood as the central and unifying premise fails to seriously address differences of race and class between women (Strickland, 1994). This universal approach has been positive in many respects, particularly in its contribution to the understanding of common experiences of oppression. However, this stance has also invited critiques arising from notions of a common experience among women that tends ignore differences within this group.

Harding (1991:177) considers there is another way to approach this problem. She argues that liberatory social movements and emanating standpoint theories centre a view of the world from its members' lives. This approach tends to ignore differences between lives and others. In this way, standpoint epistemology privileges the everyday lives of women and others that have been traditionally excluded from scientific analyses. Feminist standpoint theorists, such as Sandra Harding and Patricia Hill-Collins argue that women's construction of their experience offers a vantage point from which to understand oppression. From this perspective, women construct themselves as subjects and link their understanding of the world to their social experiences. Standpoint theories can be viewed as a loosely related set of theoretical positions, which posit central themes that appear across the discourse. First, there is an emphasis upon experience for theorising which employs the view that all knowledge claims are socially located. Second, standpoint epistemology envelopes political and emancipatory goals located in gendered power relationships. Thus, standpoint theories "attempt to articulate the ways in which 'different ways ways of knowing' or situated knowledges" are located in and derived from different types of commuities, organised by and at times in opposition to, relations of domination (Naples, 1994:41).

The emphasis upon women's embodied social experiece, as a site of knowledge has been vulnerable to charges of essentialism that tends to ignore differences between women's lives and others (Clough, 1994). It has been argued that this essentialised view of women often equates particular ways of knowing with their identities as women and this approach tends to ignore differences between lives and others.

However, standpoint theory contains 'tendencies both to ignore and to emphasise differences within the groups on which it focuses – in our case, differences between women or between men'. In this way, although there is a tendency to make general statements, they often become difficult to avoid. For example, when talking about aspects of women's lives in the plural, 'experiences' does not necessarily deflect claims of essentialism. In this regard, I agree with Hill-Collins (1986) and Harding (1991) about the strength of the valuable resource of standpoint theory in exploring the lives of black people and women located and situated within an alternative framework of analysis.

In a similar vein, notions of a common experience of oppression among black people have suggested critiques of essentialism and dogmatism of African-centred theories. Feminist theories attest to the common experience of struggle among women in many aspects of social and political life and the pressing need to rupture the complacency of conventional knowledge within academe in order to gain inclusion.

Historically, people of African descent have experienced 400 years of enslavement, colonialism and imperialism that has impelled the development of social movements in the struggle for survival and wellbeing. Therefore, while it is important to be mindful of totalising experiences of oppression it is equally important to recognise the shared and collective expressions of social and political thought that emanated from black social movements and that continue to empower black peoples in their struggle for social justice.

Another important element of this discussion is the marginalisation that has taken place in the production of knowledge located in relations of power and domination. These relationships of power and domination in academe are demonstrated in the 'silence of contemporary social science on post war liberation movements, on the way...that they have undertaken as a fundamental strategy the contestation of colonialised subjectivities, has been deafening' (Yeatman,1994:28). All knowledge is situated and guided by the perspective of the knowers. Bordo (1990:149) argues that the focus of postmodern frameworks has de-emphasised collective approaches to social oppression, and thus 'can obscure the trans-historical hierarchical patterns of white, male privilege that have informed the creation of the Western intellectual tradition'.

Moreover, Asante (1990) considers that 'all knowledge is political and culturally centred and flows from ideological commitments'. Thus it is important to recognise that all knowledges are contested for spaces and boundaries in intellectual discourse and this assertion assists our understanding of standpoint epistemologies that direct us to research and scholarship starting from the lives of black people.

In the context of the above, it is claimed that African people are too culturally diverse to invite common social and philosophical themes. These claims are made in relation to continental Africa but are relevant to African people within the diaspora. Similarly, Outlaw (1996) argues that the presentation of commonalities underlies a disregard of other factors of difference. Gyekye's (1995:191) approach refutes these notions and provides evidence of commonalities in comparative studies of traditional African social thought found in the customs, values, beliefs, traditions and historical experiences of African people.

He suggests that:

in many areas of thought we can discern features of the traditional life and thought of African peoples sufficiently common to constitute a legitimate and reasonable basis for the construction (or reconstruction) of a philosophical system that may properly be called African – African not in the sense that every African adheres to it, but in the sense that philosophical systems arise from, and hence is [sic] essentially related to, African life and thought. Such a basis would justify a discourse in terms of African philosophy.

It is precisely the disruption of traditional social ways that created discontinuity which provides the space to reconstruct a coherent system of theories in alliance with other oppressed and progressive people. This includes 'an explicit intention to separate and to analyse present constraints of African society, marking the present and future situation while remaining true to African ideals' (Outlaw, 1996:235). The sharing of distinctive experiences, enslavement and colonialisation provide an initial distinction in a field of discourse that is necessary in order to have insights into the forms, agendas, strategies, traditions and practices within the context of lived experiences and worldviews. Although there is a need to avoid conflating the quest for unity there remains a form of philosophising embedded within the historical, cultural and social experiences, visions and realities.

Black people share a common humanity anchored in the similar aspirations, hopes, pain, suffering, visions and spirituality of all human beings. However, Africans and people of African descent have a distinctive experience that has been shaped and conditioned by their encounters with Europe and their struggle to survive as a free people. These experiences are in many respects unique and clearly distinguishable from other segments of humanity. It is within this context that the 'continuity of this purposefulness across times and spaces, conditioning the very core of our being as living peoples, has been the subject of much song, writing and discussion' (Outlaw, 1996:131).

Pan-Africanism – resistance, struggle, reclamation and renewal

Expressions of social and political thought have largely been evoked within social movements that span the Caribbean, Africa and the Americas. These social movements have important connections within European/Western contexts in the civil rights movements, and are located in postcolonial struggles. Pan-African social movements have a long historical claim to unity that rests upon the separation and fragmentation engendered by the experience of enslavement and the colonial era that provided strategies for resistance, rebellion, survival and wellbeing. These social and political movements advocated unity among African people throughout the world also for spiritual as well as physical reconnection with Africa in self-defining approaches and self-determination. For example, the first Pan-African conference in London in the year 1900 set the agenda for strategies of resistance in Africa and renewal and expressed the concerns of black people in England and the Americas. These concerns involved representations to the government of the day (Fryer, 1984).

Pan-African social movements encompassed a variety of social and political thought. These variations are expressed in the definitions of Pan-Africanism. Winston located Pan-Africanism within class struggles and suggested that Pan-Africanism is 'part of the international proletarian struggle against imperialism and has its roots in a class phenomenon – the oppression of African labour by international capitalism' (cited in Chrisman, 1973:5). On the other hand, J. H. Clarke (1990) considers Pan-Africanism as a project that restores African people to their proper place in world history to bring about a unity of African people in order to reclaim what enslavement and colonialism took away.

Rodney (1974) links Pan-Africanism with the Caribbean, insisting that the Caribbean was the first area where enslaved African people were taken.

There they defined themselves as African and forged a common experience of struggle and resistance against enslavement. Their concerns were not driven by terminology or academic questions about the term 'African' but questions of survival and the amelioration of conditions of enslavement. Thus, there is a common theme of struggle, resistance and rebellion associated with renewal and reclamation within the various strands of Pan-Africanism. These aspects of Pan-Africanism provide unifying possibilities and potentialities that have informed liberation philosophy expressed in associated political and social thought. The revival of Pan-African social and political thought was an important influence in the civil rights movement in the USA and community organisations in Britain. This resulted in a shift towards establishing a cultural base as the organising principle that advocated core values of resistance, and self-determination.

The cultural base for the organising principle of unity has developed a two-pronged approach that includes a critical perspective of challenge, resistance and struggle against marginalisation and exclusion manifested in the operation of cultural hegemony. This stance also incorporates the renewal and reclamation of knowledge, including spiritual knowledge, that is often shared with societies outside European/Western contexts. The historical contexts of resistance and struggle generate a collective consciousness and spiritual sense of knowing and belongingness that adds power and strength in the everyday lives of people of African descent.

Within this arena, it is claimed that beyond race and ethnic considerations these efforts assist in identifying philosophies as characteristic of African people. For many African thinkers these shared characteristics have provided the framework of a way of articulating and understanding new identities that are not confined to the limiting situation of oppression. These identities evolve from theories that suggest 'starting off thought' from the lives of marginalised peoples; beginning in those determinate, objective locations in any social order will generate illuminating critical questions that do not arise in thought that begins from dominant group lives' (Harding, 1993:56). In this way, these identities provide the source of survival and wellbeing, thereby assisting in 'the effort to recover or reconstruct life defining, identity-confirming meaning-connections to lands and cultures of the African continent, its peoples and their histories' (Outlaw, 1996:89).

Liberation philosophy is a continuation of African intellectual history located within a theme of unity in diversity standpoint. Davidson (1991:16) traces the origins of Pan-Africanism through two major historical epochs, the emergence of an Iron Age culture and the coming of the desert to the Sahara region of Africa. He observes:

In this long and complex disintegration of the Neolithic pattern and its reconstruction within an Iron Age framework we can find the origins of modern African societies, showing as these do, in a multitude of ways a diversity that is nonetheless rooted in a profound and ancient unity.

In this way, the cultural unity of Africa rests upon a common background of an ancient cultural unity of Africa that has been identified by scholars such as Diop (1974,1991) and Obenga (1995). However, can we assume that it is possible to transpose the historical cultural unity of Africa across both time and space given the rupture of enslavement and the dispersal of people within the diaspora?

Asante (1980) proposes that there is a unity of experience, struggle and origin that causes African cultures to have an internal unity just as European culture does. Research studies located in black communities within the diaspora indicate that African cultural retentions inform the social practices, values, beliefs and social realities among African peoples (Herskovits,1958; Alleyne, 1971; Holloway, 1990). These studies point to the varying degrees of cultural retention among people of African descent that can be found in child-rearing practices, religion, language, family structures, elderhood, music and value systems. The exposition of these cultural dimensions has been viewed by some scholars as presenting an extended idea of unity that tends to present a totalising history of all African people. These dangers can be avoided by the critical appreciation of the complexities of communities and differences that emanate from the diverse geographical sources. The interrogation of these dimensions has provided the space where African identities can be voiced, validated and interrogated.

Closely related to these concerns is the dogmatism suggested by some proponents of African-centred thought, which is sometimes exploited at the expense of critical dialogue. There is clearly no one African-centred reality that can take account of class, gender and ethnic differences. As Hunter (1983:43) usefully points out, 'the belief that one's view of reality is the only reality is the most dangerous of all delusions'. In any event, African-centred epistemologies cover a broad terrain of realities that must avoid privileging one view over another. In a similar vein Asante (1990:5) contends that 'the Afrocentrist will not question the idea of centrality of African ideals and values but will argue over what constitutes those ideals and values'.

Along the same lines, critics have focused upon concerns about over-romanticising the historical African past. In any exploration of African-centred epistemology, there is a risk of romanticising or glorifying the African past, particularly in connection with pre-colonial social forma-tions. However, these critiques raise similar problems when one considers the denigration of Africa and African people in European/Western contexts. As Dei (1994:16) quite succinctly argues:

> *it is important for those who critique romanticism not to confuse the recuperation and celebration of African peoples, their historicities, and past traditions with romanticisation or glorification. I think we can have a simultaneous celebration and a serious interrogation of African cultures, cultural values and norms.*

The revival of the past has evoked discussions about the tendency towards a prescriptive normative theory within African-centred epistemologies. These norms and values ground and assist in structuring ways of life and con-tribute to a collective worldview. Some critics have challenged these knowledges and raised questions about authenticity and the failure to address issues of class, gender and ethnicity. These challenges are closely related to the limitations of normative theories that may lead to the reproduction of the very oppressions which they are intended to overcome.

There is ample evidence to support the contention that there are various forms of domination based upon gender, class and ethnic lines that existed in traditional Africa and are still apparent in African societies today (Dei, 1994). These forms of domination bring into sharp focus questions such as in what ways can African-centred epistemologies claim to be a progressive emancipatory discourse? This discussion urges African-centred theories to confront and critique the normative theories derived from its historical base. Entering into discussions concerning normative theories makes one mindful of the problematics and difficulties that are intrinsic to the field.

Outlaw (1996) argues that it is not possible for African-centred theories to set the normative agenda for African and African-descended peoples. This is because there is such a large collection of traditions and practices, agendas and literatures of African and African-descended peoples. In this discussion, the normative agenda proffered by much of African-centred social thought is grounded upon a particular set of values thought to be indigenous to the lives of black people. This enterprise has consistently been historicist in nature, and has presented a powerful critique in the struggles against the general disparagement of African people and their knowledges. These challenges raise a double-blind scenario in jettisoning normative claims to knowledge and critiques that there is no coherent body of thought which is precisely the critique that has been directed to the notions of 'black perspectives' in social welfare and social work. It has been claimed that black people do not have theories: they just have perspectives emanating from their experiences of racism. Clearly, all knowledges contain essentialism and certain key premises, even postmodernism, and thus it is generally not possible to escape these problematics. Individuals and groups can reject the way in which they are positioned in discourses and work towards the creation of new and more emancipatory discourses. However, there still remains the challenge of setting out definitive agendas and the dilemmas this approach raises.

According to Foucault, the production of truths is revealed through their discovery within a genealogical process 'that is a form of history which can account for the construction of knowledges, discourses, domains of object of objects, etc.' (cited in Gordon 1980:117). Foucault's theories allude to the problematics in raising historical monuments as a corrective to the disparagement of the past by European scholarship in an attempt to discover essential truths (Foucault, 1980). This view in turn results in Outlaw's (1996:35) conclusion that the whole enterprise was 'created in service to contemporary needs and projects...precisely to overcome discontinuities and the absence of unity'.

Although this project seeks to examine every aspect of the subject place of African people in historical, social, ethical, philosophical, economic and political life, it remains true to African ideals. These important elements of the project offer a way out of the impasse in providing sources of knowledge that can inform a critical appraisal of normative agendas and structures which assist in underwriting a coherent disciplinary field of studies. In this way, critical appraisal of normative structures and agendas can be undertaken to ascertain their sources of empowerment and disempowerment in the search for ways to strengthen their cultural heritage. This critical approach allows groups and individuals to 'reclaim the identity that the dominant culture has taught them to despise' (Young, 1990:166).

Conclusion

I have mapped the field of African-centred social thought, its contours and boundaries. In ending this discussion, African philosophy clearly operates as a frame for various strands of African social thought. These strands assist in defining the ways in which cultural identities are framed and shaped. Thus, these expressions of culture make sense of the relationship between the past and the future and give meaning to present struggles for self-determination and social justice. Philosophising on fundamental issues arises out of the need to understand, interpret and advance human existence. These considerations have inspired thinkers in all societies. European Enlightenment philosophies placed African people, women and other non-European societies outside the realms of philosophising, and in various ways they are implicated in the formation of modern racism and sexism. It is in this context that African-centred social thought seeks to interpret human existence in striving to connect theories with everyday experiences. Philosophy is not merely about some abstract meaning of life but is informed by the meaning of real lives and experiences.

African-centred social thought provides a valuable resource as universal knowledge that can in fact be local, historical, cultural and subjective. Situated knowledges, such as African-centred thought, are not committed to essentialist assumptions. The divisions in European social thought result in a choice between Enlightenment and postmodern projects. African-centred thought is poised to take a different path that acknowledges unity in diversity which has historically framed strands of African philosophy. Moreover, African philosophy shares aspects of its nature with world philosophies and complies with the notion of a multiplicity of knowledges, each of equal value that span human knowledge.

Liberation philosophy embraces knowledge-seeking from the experiences of oppression. In this way, situated knowledge is informed by histories, ways of living and experiences to provide a resource for black people as subjects and the generators of social thought. These knowledges have given meaning and sustained communities in efforts to empower black communities. They also provide valuable insights which reveal views of reality that may be obscured by more orthodox approaches (Hill-Collins, 1989).

This discussion raises the issue of relativism, implying the existence of frameworks and positions which each have their own validity or standards. In this way, critiques drawn from outside the framework can be avoided. African-centred social thought advocates a perspective which acknowledges other points of view. Thus, African-centred social thought is capable of sustaining several types of discourse. Moreover, relativism is not fundamentally a problem that emerges from any thought, which starts from the lived experiences of black peoples and other marginalised groups.

The critique of relativism is often evoked from the thought of dominant groups. Foucault (1980) considers reality as knowledge via our representations of reality. Thus our representations of reality are informed by historical and cultural variables but arise out of differences in the positioning of knowing subjects (Harding, 1991). Definitions of reality have been the source of intense debates and discussions among black scholars. These debates bring into sharp focus the location of the power to define reality and, more importantly, to have other people respond to your definition as if it were their own (Nobles, 1985). In this way, definitions of reality that are shaped and defined by Eurocentric thought and imposed on black communities and individuals are critiqued in order to rupture the complacency of conventional knowledge and construct sites and spaces of resistance.

To research from the perspective of the lived experiences of black people shifts the production of knowledge towards the very people who are trying to fit their understandings of lives within constructs that have meaning and value. These understandings are rooted in the histories and cultures of black people that demand a collective approach to the struggles against oppression and assist in making the connections between individual and collective consciousness. These considerations enable the full appreciation of human experiences steeped in substantive historical and cultural legacies.

The intense discussions and debate in this chapter are closely associated with the validity, legitimacy and authenticity of African knowledges and the degree to which they have been shaped and defined by a European heritage. However, there is no doubt about the historical nature of cultural retrieval and retention that forms an integral part of African-centred thought. Moreover, the dimensions of black consciousness that continues to assert the re-telling of African history to reveal a meaningful past that has importance for the present and future needs of black people.

It is within this context that social work can realise its core values in the expansion of its philosophical framework to advance substantive social change. A diversified philosophical base encourages social workers to view their mission in broader terms. The attributes of African-centred worldviews can be utilised by any group or individuals interested in pursuing social work approaches that insist upon spirituality, humanism, cultural resource knowledge and human possibilities in designing effective interventions.

Chapter 5
A critical analysis of existing models of social work

Social work interventions with black families and children have been the source of controversy, conflict and disquiet for many decades. Research evidence continues to indicate that black communities are over-represented in those services that involve social control functions: for example, the juvenile justice system in its dealings with young black people, compulsory admissions to psychiatric units, and child protection. Black families are under-represented in receiving preventative and supportive aspects of service delivery (Rowe and Lambert, 1982; NACRO, 1991, Skellington and Morris, 1992; Barn, 1993; Roys, 1993).

The Association of Black Social Workers and Allied Professions (ABSWAP) provided compelling evidence to the House of Commons Select Committee in 1983 highlighting the plight of black children in the care system and was active in identifying the need for a legislative framework which addressed race, culture and language in the provision and delivery of services (ABSWAP, 1983). Despite the introduction of the 1989 Children Act, and in particular, Section 22 (5) C which clearly requires local authorities to give due consideration to 'the child's religious persuasion, racial origin and cultural and linguistic background' in the provision of services and service delivery, black children of all ages and both sexes continue to be over-represented in the public care system.

Institutional racism has been identified as one of the main instigators in the continued oppression of black communities in society and its effects are compounded by 'the system' of social welfare (Ahmad, 1990; Dominelli, 1997). The primary response of social work in addressing the needs of black people has been to adapt existing models of social work with special attention given to racism and cultural differences. The ethnic-sensitive model in the USA and anti-discriminatory practice (which now incorporates anti-racist practice) have emerged as the most appropriate paradigms to assist and meet their needs.

At this juncture it is useful to consider the pathway advocated by several black researchers in placing the capacities of black families at the forefront of theoretical explanations, therapeutic ideas and research models. Notwithstanding the critical debates surrounding the strengths of black families are discussed in Chapter 2, Barbara Solomon's book *Black Empowerment, Social Work in Oppressed Communities*, remains an influential text in shifting dominant psycho-dynamic approaches in social work toward an examination of the complex structural and institutional forces that can generate social problems in society.

The purpose of this chapter is, first, to examine anti-racist and ethnic-sensitive approaches to social work. While these models have been useful in highlighting forms of structural disadvantage arising from oppressive institutions and practices and cultural considerations in social work with black families, limited attention has been paid to their inherent limitations. These limitations are located within frameworks of adaptation or modification that serve to mask theoretical deficits found within the ethnocentric nature of conventional social work knowledge. Moreover, anti-racist and ethnic-sensitive models of social work make insufficient use of cultural resource knowledge as paradigms for social work practice.

Second, we shall be articulating the strengths of black families as identified by several black scholars as the basis for empowerment models of social work. Third, we shall examine Solomon's (1976) empowerment model of social work and explore its purposeful elements shared by African-centred models and approaches. Finally, we shall study models of social work in black communities. These insights will serve to provide the context and background against which to consider the broadening of conceptual knowledge in social work.

The theoretical frameworks that inform social work practice with black families

In response to the growing awareness that traditional social work models have been ineffective and oppressive in addressing the needs of African people, ethnic-sensitive social work practice in the USA and anti-discriminatory practice (which now incorporates anti-racist practice) in the UK have been proposed as the way forward in providing the 'blueprint' for good social work practice with black people. The model of anti-racist social work is predicated upon theories drawn from the sociology of race relations to provide an understanding of the source and impact of different kinds of inequality and oppression. Dominelli, (1988), Thompson (1993) and Ahmad (1990) define racism as an ideological social construct that involves social and political meanings culminating in 'the belief in the inherent superiority of one race over all others and thereby the right to dominance' (Lorde, 1984:115). The social effects of racism are manifested in disadvantage that permeates areas of social life, housing, employment, education and so on. Thus, the understanding of the social construct of race and racism becomes central to the anti-racist discourse as a tool to organise for social change.

The dominant anti-racist and anti-discriminatory practice focus and parameters of this model are expressed as follows:

- understanding how racism, oppression and discrimination have created barriers to opportunities in the wider society, agencies and structures

- social worker awareness of personal biases, attitudes and stereotypes; challenges to racism within others and institutions (Thompson, 1993; Schiele, 1994).

Social services' response to the latter objective of this model during the 1980s included 'race' awareness training, which has been the centre of debate and has been heavily criticised for producing over-simplified solutions to complex social phenomena. Moreover, the anti-racist approach was vilified as 'silly' and irresponsible and inappropriate to social work. These attacks were endorsed within academic circles as questions were raised about its ideological base paradoxes and muddle located within the concept of race (Macey and Moxon, 1996). For example, it was argued that sociologists generally disagree about what single theoretical perspective could adequately analyse and explain racism in Britain. Moreover, theoretical perspectives derived from sociological explanations of race tend to present a simplistic view in addressing questions of service provision and delivery (Macey and Moxon, 1996). These concerns sparked off a tirade of attacks upon social work education from the New Right and within academic circles dedicated to 'rooting out politically correct nonsense' (Greenwood, 1993, cited in Macey and Moxon, 1996).

This critique of theoretical models of 'race' fails to acknowledge that race is more than a theoretical concept: 'it is also an idea that governs social relations'. Moreover, some of problematics identified in the constructs of 'race' can be ascribed to what Dei (1999b) terms intellectual gymnastics born out of a liberal position that denies the saliency of race as irrelevant, yet evokes its relevance when expedient both at the same time. For example, many educators and academics simply equate race with ethnicity to counter the importance of race in discussions about school exclusions. However, interestingly, but disturbingly 'race' is evoked in public and academic discussions about crime and the problem of young black people (Dei, 1996, Graham, 2001). Nevertheless, despite the problematics identified in the theoretical constructs of race, Dominelli (1988:71–2) provides several useful strategies that may be adopted by practitioners which often work against the establishment of anti-racist working practices.

1. A denial that racism exists, particularly in its cultural and institutional forms. Practitioners utilising this strategy often view racism as personal prejudice held by a few extreme and irrational individuals.

2. The dynamics of racism played out in everyday social interactions are neglected. Individuals subscribing to this view do not see the relevance of race in most situations, and relate to others as if racism did not exist.

3. Dominelli uses the term decontextualisation to describe the way that people acknowledge the existence of racism outside their immediate society (for example, in the USA or South Africa) but refuse to accept that racism permeates aspects of British society.

4. This strategy takes the form of denying that racism exists in organisations and individuals, often based upon the premise of treating everyone the same and supporting a view of assimilation. Race and colour are rendered insignificant and patterns of discrimination ignored.

5. A strategy identified as the 'dumping' approach. Here, the responsibility for racism is placed upon black people and it is incumbent upon them to challenge and act against racist practices. Thus the victims of racism are blamed for what happens.

6. A patronising approach to black people where superiority of cultural values and ways of life prevail. Although there is superficial acceptance of black people and their cultural values and traditions, these are tolerated within a context of inferiority, which permeates social work processes and practices.

7. The strategy of avoidance where there is an awareness of race as a factor. However, practitioners shy away from opportunities to confront it and so the contentious issue of race is avoided.

In this context, anti-discriminatory practice tries to put social work's 'house in order' in attempts to combat racism in the system and within the 'professional' subjective judgements of social workers. Anti-discriminatory practice is concerned with limiting the damage within social work practice that preaches the worth of every individual yet supports institutional and cultural racism at every level. The underlying knowledge base of anti-discriminatory practice is confined within the parameters of this essentially reactive stance against racism and oppression that often minimises the complexity and richness of black experiences. The existing parameters of anti-discriminatory practice do not provide social work models that aspire to support, nurture and understand the emotional, spiritual and developmental needs of black families in advancing the collective interests of black people.

Instead, this social work model promotes damage limitation by positing a 'black perspective/experience' which is articulated as an adaptation or modification of existing theoretical frameworks that serves to mask more fundamental theoretical deficits inherent within the ethnocentric nature of social work knowledge. Consequently, this model falls short of creating a social work that mirrors the worldview and cultural values of those who are most often recipients of social work interventions. Moreover, as Karenga (1997:34) wrote, 'a people whose paradigms of thought and practice are borrowed from its oppressor clearly have limited human possibilities'. Creativity and transformation are available when the individual is connected to his or her cultural context.

Anti-discriminatory practice offers the potential of a response that is 'free' from discrimination on several levels but falls short of providing a knowledge base for social work that is engaged in the collective development of the black community. As Williams (1999:214) argues:

> *[this] predominant approach trivialises and minimises much of the richness of black experience by presenting it simply as a reaction to white domination. This tendency to present black people's lives as problematic and to confer victim status upon them has been particularly noticeable in much of social work literature.*

Moreover, many commentators have argued that the term 'black perspectives' lacks conceptual clarity. Macey and Moxon (1996) ask 'Which black perspective and whose black voice?' These questions raise concerns about definitions of the term 'black' and also cultivate the idea that black people have perspectives rather than valid knowledge and theories. In this context, the notion of black perspectives becomes vulnerable to critique because perspectives are defined by the above authors as 'listening to their experiences and having these inform practice' and in so doing is defined in terms of 'no more than good social work' (Macey and Moxon, 1996:305). These insights draw attention to the limiting nature of Eurocentric epistemologies and derived helping models. These limitations will come under closer scrutiny as there is now greater awareness of the possibilities and potentialities within new lines of thinking and human experiences.

Ethnic-sensitive social work: an expression of cultural oppression?

Multiculturalism has generated a wealth of literature defining multicultural approaches in social work and texts articulating cross-cultural practice. These perspectives are derived from theories of cultural pluralism as a central feature of its discourse.

Kincheloe and Steinberg (1997:1) refer to multiculturalism as a used and misused term surrounded by an array of meanings including a code word for 'race' or a term evoking derision and ridicule; indeed, a term that is 'everything and at the same time nothing'.

The dominant view of multiculturalism is based upon integration, in the sense that minoritised groups should be given the opportunity to participate in the social, economic and political life of society coupled with the maintenance of their own cultural heritage and its institutions. Conventional social work approaches were largely based upon deficit models that identified cultural values and traditions as the locus of problems and 'deviant' behaviours. The shift away from constructs of deviancy and pathology towards strengths and cultural sensitivity demonstrate a wide acceptance of ethnic sensitivity or cultural competence approaches to practice. Moreover, there has been an emphasis upon approaches that 'cut across the various groups, identifying universals and making the bewildering, array of differences more manageable' (Pinderhughes, 1994:271). This is the case in the cultural-sensitive models advocated by Pinderhughes (1994) and Devore and Schlesinger (1991).

Ethnic sensitivity, cultural diversity and cross-cultural practice have entered conventional social work as new language, seemingly located outside the realms of assimilation. However, upon closer examination, models of social work ensconced in the language of pluralism and diversity reveal a new take on a familiar theme.

Pinderhughes (1994) outlines several important concepts that are regarded as essential for social workers to enable them to practise effectively within a culturally sensitive framework and context with black and minoritised groups. These concepts include appreciation, knowledge and respect for cultural values; systems theory; being comfortable with difference and power configurations; and flexibility in thinking and behaviour. Developing these skills is an important preparation for social workers.

Critics of this approach have drawn attention to its focus upon cultural factors and individual change that ignores or pays little attention to structural contingencies and power relationships. Within the USA context, research indicates ethnic-sensitive services have led to mostly marginal and symbolic changes in organisations (Gutierrez and Nagda, 1996). Despite the rhetoric and new language, ethnic-sensitive models in social work are mainstream.

The ethnic-sensitive model advocated by Devore and Schlesinger (1991:49) proposes the need for 'sensitivity' to cultural differences, together with an understanding and appreciation of racial, cultural and social diversity. According to this model there is an infusion of cultural differences and nuances into existing models of social work practice. This model is based upon the concept of 'ethnic reality'. This reality generates identifiable characteristics and behaviours that arise out of a 'group's cultural values as these are embodied in its history, rituals and religion; a group's migration experience or other processes through which the encounter with the mainstream culture took place; the way a group organises its family systems'.

The model provides specific strategies that include:

- awareness of and sensitivity to cultural differences and value systems of ethnic and cultural groups
- adaptation to practice skills in response to the differing family patterns and life styles
- an understanding of how cultural traditions and values influence family functioning and consider these nuances in planning social work interventions

The concept of ethnic reality is placed within a social work knowledge base, which is inherently ethnocentric. As F. J. Turner (1986:2) maintains, 'theory builds a series of propositions about reality; that is it provides us with models of reality and helps us to understand what is possible and how we can attain it'.

In other words, the 'reality' of black people is placed within the realities of others who have constructed their own theories and models of practice as the basis for solving people's problems. Somehow, it is assumed that these will provide the principal remedies for black oppression and for problems within black families and communities. Asante (1987:165) asks the poignant question, 'How can the oppressed use the same theories as the oppressors?'

The levels of adaptation of prevailing models of social work practice to the infusion of the ethnic reality is the key theme in the social work literature; the fact that the prevailing models of social work practice are an expression of the hegemony of Eurocentric knowledge is ignored.

According to Devore and Schlesinger (1991:187) they 'do not presume to generate a new body of practice strategies and procedures', but suggest how traditional social work models might be adjusted or adapted in keeping with ethnic reality.

The ethnic-sensitive approach uncovers several flaws that contribute to a projected image of the 'universality' of existing social work paradigms and, more importantly, the establishment of the social work knowledge base as the norm. This model maintains a subtle form of cultural oppression in negating the legitimacy of other worldviews as the basis for social work theory and practice.

As Schiele (1997:803) argues, cultural oppression 'is achieved by imposing one group's culture onto another's in a manner that marginalises and devalues the culture of another'. In other words, the knowledge validation and hegemony in information dissemination cannot be separated from social, political and economic hegemony within British institutions and the wider society. Nobles and Goddard (1985:27), leading Afrocentric scholars, identify the control element propagated within traditional social science paradigms:

The most efficient way to keep black people oppressed and powerless is to provide them with ideas that justify and certify our status and condition. A powerful approach to the empowerment of marginalised groups is to work together to develop critical consciousness, to develop together the tools to critique frames of reference, ideas, information, and patterns of privilege.

The hegemonic nature of social work knowledge propagates the belief that Eurocentric precepts are primary in the analysis of social problems because they are presented as devoid of cultural impositions that affect the theorist and theorising, thereby suggesting objectivity in the understanding of human behaviour. This expression of cultural oppression in social work fosters the belief that black people lack the skills and abilities to develop social work designs. These beliefs must be challenged by African-centred social work educators and other critical theorists in order to gain cultural inclusion, and a anti-racist model in social work must consider how race and gender are implicated in ways of knowing and of knowledge itself.

Strengths and empowerment models of black families

As mentioned in an earlier chapter, the strengths of black families have served as the source of empowerment models of social work. The shift away from deficit models of black families emerged as a chorus of black scholars and researchers challenged problem-orientated frameworks to identify strengths inherent within black families in advocating a positive perspective for practice (Billingsley, 1968; R. Hill, 1972; Macdonald, 1991). Despite the problematics surrounding the concept of strengths, this approach promotes collaboration and partnership and embodies the potential to shift power relationships between social worker and client and assist communities to gain greater control over the ways in which services are designed and delivered.

Strengths have been defined as 'those traits which facilitate the ability of the family to meet the needs of its members and the demands made upon it by systems outside the family unit. They are necessary for the survival and maintenance of effect family networks' (R. Hill 1971:3).

Black scholars, such as Hill, 1972 have identified and articulated strengths of black families in the following ways.

1. *Survival of black families* – Historically, black families have survived the distinctive forces such as enslavement and colonialisation that have sought to destroy black family life. The continued prescence of black families is testament to their enduring strengths and a cause for celebration. Akbar (1985:27) captures the resilience of black people in the face of deep-seated racism and oppression when he declares 'our very presence as effectively functioning scholars, fathers, mothers, citizens, [and] scientists actually defies . . . theories of human development.

2. *Strong religious and spiritual orientation* – spirituality is a common cultural value framing the worldviews of black peoples throughout the world. There is an acceptance of a non-material higher force present in all life's affairs. Expression of spirituality has often taken place in religious organisations and these social practices have been identified as key factors in sustaining families, promoting resilience, and nurturing spiritual values and as a source of creativity Bryan *et al.*, (1985:132) draws attention to the importance of black churches in helping people to cope with stressful events. They write:

   The churches provided black women with one of our main sources of support and sustenance, offering some continuity with the forms of social and community organisation we have known in the Caribbean. For many of us, these churches offered the only form of recreation we had to relieve the pressures of our working lives, and to support an otherwise bleak existence ...It is in the church communities too that the origins of some of our earliest social and welfare organisations are to be found.

3. *Strong achievement orientation*
   Black families have traditionally placed great value upon education and knowledge. Black parents have rejected the limitations placed upon their children by educational systems. The importance of education in black communities has been explained as a way of

counteracting the effects of oppression and discrimination. The desire for education is sometimes expressed within a vision of the future where all things are possible in life and human potential has no external boundaries. These socialisation patterns provide an overarching framework to the acquisition of knowledge and educational attainment grounded in community consciousness and understanding (Mirza and Reay, 2000).

4. *Strong kinship bonds*
   In traditional societies, all family members were involved in the parenting process. The community shared responsibility for all children: children belonged to the community. Older siblings and significant others are an integral part of the parenting process (Chestang, 1974). Concepts of family include members who are not biologically related, including an extensive network of cousins. The concept of illegitimacy is generally unknown, so all children are legitimate. Families have traditionally adopted children informally and these children retain their names as an important link to their lineage and kinship to their biological parents.

5. *A tradition of communal self-help* has featured as an integral part of the African cultural value systems. Self-help is built upon notions of exchange and reciprocity which are active social patterns found in black communities.
   According to Dei (1994) there were many indigenous forms of mutual self-help groups in traditional African societies: for example, self-loaning groups such as *susu* among the Akan of Ghana (Goody, 1962) and *ensusu* among the Yoruba of Nigeria (Bascom, 1952). The vestiges of these forms of mutual help are evident and continue to play an important part in the lives of black communities in Britain today. Self-loaning groups known as *susu* and *pardner* were popular forms of generating resources to ensure economic survival for many black families on low incomes and afforded the opportunity for others to purchase homes during the 1960s and 1970s. Bryan *et al.* (1985:131) explains the 'pardner system':

   Most significantly we organised the Pardner system through which we saved regularly and collectively. By withdrawing the money we pooled on a rota basis, we gave ourselves access to much needed funds...Whoever's needs were greater, they got the deposit on a house. It was the woman who held on to the money and paid down the deposit, but still no home could be put in her name. Later people started to have selling parties. It helped to pay the mortgage, but it also provided us with somewhere to go.

6. *The adaptability of family roles to new social structures and environments* was another key factor in survival. This approach to family functioning includes the sharing of responsibility and decision-making to meet the needs of the family. This orientation towards flexibility in performance of family roles may involve for example, older siblings caring for younger siblings. The positive attempts of black fathers to rear their children have received relatively little attention in academic circles, and you will rarely find descriptions of the positive contributions made by fathers in promoting the wellbeing of their children. The neglect of this area of much needed research may be linked to the lack of worth and value accorded to black men generally and the prevalence of social science research devoted to widely held perceptions of their pathological and deviant behaviours.

Strengths and empowerment models in social work

The adoption of a strengths-based model of black families has been embraced by social work literature and widely accepted within the profession. The strengths perspective serves as the basis for developing empowerment models for practice. These models draw upon a strengths approach in harnessing both inner and outer resources as an effective way to address the needs of black families and communities. Solomon (1987:81) endorses this approach by advancing empowerment as a means of 'acknowledging and enhancing the strengths that have been the basis for survival of black families despite tremendous suffering and hardship'. The strengths approach draws upon the view that humans have the inherent capacity for growth and change. Therefore, it is the qualities within individuals and families that have facilitated their survival in the face of challenges in life, thus providing a useful source of capacity building. In this way, individuals and families are encouraged to 'define and ascribe meaning to their own situations' (Early and GlenMaye, 2000:119). In this context, the life worlds of individuals and families become the frame of reference and main focus in the helping process. Thus, charting the strengths of black families provides the conceptual framework to develop models of social work practice.

A review of social work literature provides several definitions of empowerment closely linked to conventional notions of power and power relationships. Although there is no general agreement about the definition of empowerment in social work, it is possible to elicit a consensus in the commitment of the profession in the following ways: first, by assisting people to acquire increased power and capacity to influence forces that affect and determine the quality of life; and second, by assisting individuals and groups to assert their social welfare needs in bringing about social change in power relationships.

Browne (1995) reviews empowerment practice and identifies its characteristics in three ways. First of all, Solomon (1976), who originally introduced empowerment into social work practice, describes empowerment as an intervention and strategy. For Solomon (1976), empowerment involves both traditional and creative approaches to practice in order to effect social change. Empowerment as an intervention and strategy requires social workers to acquire specific skills and responsibilities.

Second, empowerment has been characterised as a process in which social workers help clients to help themselves. This approach places emphasis upon individual empowerment acquired through capacity to influence and control external forces (Pinderhughes, 1989).

Gutierrez's (1997) approach to empowerment as a process includes interventions that support individual empowerment as a contribution to the overall empowerment of communities and societal change. According to Gutierrez (1997:251), the process of empowerment can take place 'when practice methods are focused upon education, participation, and capacity building'. Community empowerment then enhances the functioning of individual members. Third, empowerment can also be seen as a form of advocacy that lends itself to mediation in social work.

Feminist scholars define empowerment in ways both similar to and different from those found in social work literature (Browne, 1995). The varying operational mechanisms of empowerment underlie the major paradigms of feminism. Feminist notions of empowerment as a process consider the personal as the political. Empowerment takes place through consciousness-raising groups and networks and social action. Feminists critically appraise what constitutes a social problem and the ways in which patriarchal social relations operate to shape and define women's oppression. Butler and Wintram (1991) believe that it is important to articulate experiences of women to increase the visibility of all women. They argue that it is only when this has been accomplished that feminists can grapple with differences between women and the interplay of race, disability, age and sexuality. Butler and Wintram (1991:15) view women's empowerment as a celebration of womanhood where women can take power for themselves and use these energies in a positive way towards human growth and social change. Empowerment 'involves an exploration of the interstitial and spreading branches of women's diversity', and in this way it can build bridges 'between women separated by social inequality'. In Lee's (1994:109) view, 'empowerment takes place as we make a common cause with each other and as we withdraw our silent assent to oppressive conditions and actively value and promote human liberation'. Liberation is a process that implies working for empowerment. This process involves campaigns, networks and activism within the political and public spheres of life. Dominelli and Macleod (1989) demonstrate the varying ways in which consciousness-raising has spearheaded new initiatives in advancing women's welfare generally: for example, women's refuges, health-care facilities, employment and child-care. Empowerment, then, as both a process and strategy, emerges along varying trajectories according to definitions of power and explanations for the cause and effect of women's oppression.

Solomon (1976) developed a model of empowerment as a process and intervention strategy for social work practice. Solomon (1976) criticised psychologically-based methods of social work as ineffective and ideologically suspect in working with black communities. The preoccupation of social work in effecting change in individual functioning served to compound racism and oppression. Solomon (1976) recognised the potential for change within institutions, the corrosive impact of oppression and racism within the wider society upon individuals and families, and the need to bridge the gap between the micro and macro level.

The focus on the individual and his or her failings, coupled with an adaptation model of practice relegating social barriers and the impact of wider society to the periphery in social work interventions, conspired to offer a damaging and debilitating service to black families.

Solomon proposed that negative valuations placed upon black people by wider society and, as a consequence of this process, direct and indirect power blocks, evoked powerlessness as a consequence of membership of a stigmatised group. This sense of powerlessness is affirmed and reinforced by society in subtle ways by blaming the victims (W. Ryan, 1971) through the dynamics of social relationships and social science literature. The effects of powerlessness are felt on many different levels and strategies are needed to address both individual and institutional structures. Solomon (1976) identifies direct and indirect power blocks, operating both directly and indirectly, that work together and independently in subjugating black communities.

111

Direct power blocks are located in society's major institutions where discrimination is incorporated and operationalised in its day to day activities. Indirect power blocks bring the impact and effects of racism and discrimination into the personal sphere where negative valuations become incorporated into family processes and restrict the development of personal resources. Solomon (1976) identifies the interacting and interlocking system of power blocks experienced by individuals and families, and recognises that powerlessness operates in complex ways, but argues that racism and discrimination decrease the power of the individual to deal effectively with psychosocial problems. Therefore, powerlessness is defined as an inability to obtain and utilise resources to achieve individual and collective goals. In other words, powerlessness is manifested as an inability to develop interpersonal or technical skills because of low self-esteem, which in turn reduces the individual's effectiveness in performing valued social roles. In this context, notions of power and powerlessness are related to human growth and development. This is because experiences of powerlessness 'can impinge' 'upon the individual at any step in the complex developmental process ... it may act indirectly or directly to decrease the individual's power to deal effectively with problems that arise in the course of his life' (Solomon (1976:17)

According to Solomon (1976:19), empowerment involves the implementation of specific strategies aimed at reducing the effects of indirect power blocks or the operation of direct power blocks. Empowerment is defined 'as a process whereby the social worker engages in a set of activities with the client or client system that aim to reduce the powerlessness that has been created by negative valuations based upon membership of a stigmatised group'. Solomon suggests the operationalisation of empowerment practice in advocating guiding principles and identifying the skills needed to achieve individual and collective goals. These skills are identified in the following ways:

- helping the client to perceive himself or herself as causal agent in achieving a solution to his or her problem or problems

- helping the client to perceive the social worker as having knowledge and skills which he or she can use

- helping the client to perceive the social worker as a peer collaborator or partner in the problem-solving effort

- helping the social worker to perceive the oppressive social institution (schools, social services, etc.) as open to influence to reduce negative impact

Solomon (1976) conceives empowerment practice as a method consistent with existing helping interventions, but this method helps to shift the emphasis away from treatment models to the social and increasing a family's own capacity to deal with difficulties and problems.

Moreover, Solomon (1976) addresses an important question for social workers: namely, is service delivery itself an obstacle course or an opportunity system? According to Solomon (1976), the central theme of empowerment assumes:

the experience of belonging to a stigmatised group leads to differential attitude sets and response sets in turn lead to modification of goals and social work interventions which have been based upon the dominant society's norms. Therefore, the history and unique set of experiences of the group are as important as the history of the individual – two histories influence social work interventions.

These experiences of racism and oppression are explored by the social worker to ascertain the extent to which powerlessness expressed by the individual originates from membership of a stigmatised group.

Questions about the life experiences of the individual and family and perceptions about the possibilities of change located within the outcome of interactions with social institutions are suggested in this model. Solomon suggests that the 'psychological as well as the social wellbeing of ... people is inextricably intertwined with their complex relationship with larger social institutions', which are often the primary source of the powerlessness that impairs psychological as well as social functioning. The formal and informal support systems within black communities are also explored as possible sources of empowerment.

This model of empowerment has been useful in highlighting deficiencies within traditional problem-solving models as regards moving beyond person variables as the main focus of intervention to system variables: the person in society. Moreover, this approach identifies the interaction and interlocking system of power blocks that work together and on their own in generating powerlessness. Therefore, this approach engages multiple experiences of oppression that imply the need to consider multifaceted interventions, as any single intervention 'is by itself inadequate to mitigate direct and indirect power blocks' (Harvey and Rauch, 1997:32). Insights such as these have directed Solomon (1987) to call for non-traditional social work approaches orientated towards social transformation and social change.

However, Solomon's thesis of empowerment is limited by its containment within existing models of social work. Thus, this model can be (and has been) transposed into existing models in an attempt to adapt and change the traditional relationship between professional social workers and clients. In addition, this approach supports the notions of acculturation and assimilation as it presupposes that black families share mainstream cultural values, although the process of empowerment practice creates opportunities for black people to express their own narratives as the history of the client and the collective experience of black people forms an important part of designing interventions. These interventions are restricted by the boundaries of Eurocentric knowledge forms. Therefore, it is within this context that African-centred social work models assist in shifting the focus away from dysfunction and treatment to social transformation when helping families and young people to find solutions to problems in their everyday lives. Solomon's thesis neglects this important source of empowerment that transcends racism and oppression to embrace black communities' own interpretative frameworks in designing social work interventions and strategies. Thus African-centred ways of knowing derived from cultural heritage and lived experiences are important sites of empowerment where cultural connections are made relevant to everyday experiences.

Empowerment in many black communities means liberation from oppressive barriers and control. This is experienced in various ways and situations and predicated upon a critical consciousness and a sense of rising up, determination and vision to change one's situation and predicament as a collective exercise. Empowerment invites new thinking about the challenges faced by black communities and the wider society. The starting place for new strategies and interventions has to be within communities themselves where groups and organisations are involved in attempting to address the pressing needs of families and individuals in various ways.

According to Lee (1994), empowerment invites the maintenance of culture as a strategy that embraces the importance of ideas, customs networks, skills, arts and language of a people rejecting the emphasis upon acculturation and loss. Dei (1999c:9) suggests that cultural resource knowledge provides the vehicle for affirming humanity and resistance to the severing of the past, history and cultures from black communities themselves. In this way, empowerment stands in opposition to the subordination of cultural knowledge and fosters 'the insurrection of subjugated knowledges' (Foucault, 1977, cited in Schiele, 2000).

Critical consciousness promotes critical knowledge acquisition as the tool of empowerment. Many black communities, organisations and groups have embraced cultural resource knowledge as the basis of community regeneration and theories of social change. These interpretative frameworks speak to the need to identify and explain sociocultural barriers that place all people at risk of experiencing social problems regardless of race and ethnicity. (Schiele, 2000) This space provides the domain where the falsehoods that have been told about black people and the idea 'that others know and understand them better than they know and understand themselves' can be challenged (Dei, 1999b:9).

Embracing cultural resource knowledge: models of social work in black communities

Black-led organisations and groups have often been viewed as separatist and this stance has frequently evoked negative responses from mainstream authorities. Interestingly, these concerns have been largely absent from views about other interest groups such as women's organisations, which have been accepted as legitimate and valid by the wider society (Phillips, 1982). However, black community groups have continued to assert their right to organise and unite around common interests that often embrace linkages with black organisations throughout the diaspora. Gilroy (1993) perceives black organisations as embedded in notions of blackness that are essentialist. These areas of contention have been discussed in Chapter 4. However, whilst Gilroy's (1993) thesis on the multiple identities of black people in the diaspora brings to the fore important issues about the problematic understanding of essentialised notions of blackness, his thesis fails to engage in the struggles of black communities and organisations in negotiating the linkages of culture and race in their environments. Moreover, as Gilroy (1993:45) quite succinctly declares 'the distinctive historical experiences of this diaspora's population have created a unique body of reflections on modernity and its discontents which is an enduring presence in the cultural and political struggles of their descendants today'.

For black communities these reflections are sometimes marginalised or suppressed. It is within this context that cultural knowledge as a mode of resistance has been pivotal in dislodging strategies of domination in the subjugation of the histories, cultures and experiences of black communities. Moreover, maintaining cultural resource knowledge ensures that identities and histories are not obliterated (Graham, 2001). This approach seeks to explore elements within cultural systems that can be utilised to empower communities. Therefore, it is important not only to identify and build upon these 'strengths' but to support and enhance the need for communities to institutionalise their cultural values beyond the scope of family and friends. As Schiele (1997:813) asserts, the right to self-determination and institutional development 'is nothing more than the formalisation and institutionalisation of a group's values and its political interests by establishing organisations, controlled by that group, that speak to and integrate those values and that promote that group's interests'.

Saturday and supplementary schools are time-honoured institutions that emerged in the 1960s to provide the vehicle for black parents to mobilise community resources. Black parents felt that racism within the educational system conspired to provide an environment that was hostile to their children's learning and was ultimately responsible for the under-achievement, disengagement and disaffection of their children. These concerns were confirmed in research undertaken by Dove (1990), in which parents spoke succinctly about racism being the major influence in their decision to send their children to supplementary schools.

Dove (1990) categorised parents' responses and the following is a brief summary of their motives.

● to improve their children's academic performance

● to receive more cultural learning

● to pass on black/Afrikan history

● to offer a better learning environment

● to access more support for children and parents

● to provide positive role models

● to keep children off the streets and involve them in something positive

● to build children's confidence

● to promote relationships with other black children

Parents identified social support and the role of cultural knowledge as important factors in the education of their children. Dove's (1990, 1998) survey of supplementary schools in London revealed levels of critical consciousness among parents and a recognition of the important need for their children to experience culturally affirming environments. Parents intellectualised about the impact of subtle forms of racism and its corrosive effects across various dimensions of their lives including material, social, spiritual and psychological aspects. In this context, the importance of African humanity and connections with cultural roots is affirmed and nurtured as a protective factor in the wellbeing of children.

These concerns are expressed in a series of powerful narratives:

I really understand the value of being able to have a child in a school where ultimately she learns about herself and her ancestry. It is very obvious to me, a lot of the problems we are having with our youth today is because they don't really know who they are and it happens through the public school system because they don't really work to help us know who we are ... I've had two other children go through the public school system and I just know what it does to them. (Dove, 1998:228)

It's such a struggle in this society. I mean, I've seen kids who dis their parents and dis their culture and have nothing to do with black people and that is totally sad. Even people who go to university, you know. Although these people go to do Caribbean studies, most of them are totally ... up. I don't want my kids to ever be ashamed of who they are and where they've come from. (1998:229)

In supplementary schools, learning was conveyed to the younger generation as an integral part of the community's social, spiritual/ancestral and natural environment. These schools provide a multifaceted approach that embraces pupils' social, spiritual and moral development steeped in cultural resource knowledges. Supplementary and Saturday schools have been one of the most important and enduring community institutions, yet they have been largely ignored by the mainstream (John, 1999). Similarly, social welfare activities and models of social work in black communities are relegated to the margins as if completely irrelevant to the lives of black people. In recent years there has been growing interest in African-centred theories that embrace a Caribbean past through the popularity of Kwanzaa and rites of passage programmes. Sudbury (1997) suggests that many black scholars have failed to speak accessibly about the concerns of black communities. These concerns have found expression in the ever-increasing numbers of black people who attend the Black Child Conference organised by the Kemet Educational Guidance group in Manchester, and similar annual events throughout Britain.

African-centred knowledge as a theory of social change has been the impetus for some communities to institutionalise their cultural values beyond the scope of families and friends (Graham, 2000). This approach has been evident in the growth of community rites of passage programmes in Britain as a method of supporting major transitional relationships in families and facilitating the regeneration of communities (Graham, 1987, 1999; Hill, 1992; Obonna, 1996).

There are several forms of rites of passage programmes, as outlined below.

1. Community-based rites of passage. These programmes offer short-term intergenerational rites of passage experience for young people to assist in the passage to the threshold of adulthood.

2. Church-based rites of passage programmes. These programmes have been developed alongside church orientated youth programmes.

3. Therapeutic rites of passage programmes. These programmes have been developed as social work interventions that seek to educate and support young people involved in self-destructive behaviours.

4. Family supported rites of passage programmes. Family support is provided in the transition to adulthood and includes young people, adults and elders.

Social welfare concerns about young people within black communities has provided the impetus to consider the need for an orderly process of maturation to prepare young people for adulthood. The transition of young black people into adulthood is particularly fraught within British society. Many young black people have been indoctrinated by the 'street culture' (encouraged by the media and viewed by society as 'black' culture), racist propaganda and racist images and stereotypes.

African-centred social work approaches in these programmes embrace the concept of personhood through the process of becoming that is achieved through understanding and appreciating self, community, co-operation, purpose, creativity and spirituality. This path of self-empowerment incorporates the spiritual/ancestral realms of personhood in nurturing the emotional wellbeing of young people to create new visions for families and communities. In this way, young people are challenged to grow, change and develop whilst grounded in the moral, intellectual and social virtues and ideals that are integrated within the context of local communities. These action-orientated programmes assist young people in affirming African values through patterns of interpreting reality outside the Eurocentric lines of social thought that have often located black people within a consciousness of racism and oppression. This approach gives opportunities for young black people to connect and create a way of being and thinking that is congruent with African value systems.

Hill (1992) has identified the ways in which Western societies have largely abandoned the social markers that served to delineate and define the unique transition from childhood into adulthood. Although specific language expressions defining adolescence such as 'youth', 'teenager' and 'juvenile' remain in common usage, there are few collective methods to assist young people through this life transition. According to Stevens (1982) mainstream culture has abdicated responsibility for initiating young people. People are no longer sure of which values should be passed on or why young people should be initiated. These ceremonies and transitional processes are often regarded as archaic and outmoded in contemporary society.

Hill (1992) maintains that the nearest modern version of traditional socialisation processes is to be found in formal and institutional education. The modern and ancient socialisation processes are compulsory and attempt to teach discipline and the basics of proper behaviour. Moreover, they express and communicate a worldview and central value system of culture and prepare young people for participation in wider society. Hill (1992:64) outlines the characteristics of old and new rites as follows:

- the old rites were religious; the new rites are usually secular

- the old rites ran by sun and seasonal time (outdoor and active); the new rites operate by clock and calendar (usually sedentary and pursued behind closed doors)

- the old rites provided physical risks and danger; the new rites substitute organised sports, which combine moderate challenge and minimal risk

- the old rites were dramatic, intense, forceful and fast; the new rites are slow, strung out, and often vague about the ultimate decision

- the old rites engendered awe; the new rites commonly produced detachment and boredom

- the old rites resulted in an immediate and unmistakable status change; the new rites provide no such direct deliverance into adult roles and status

- the old rites were over at a determined place and at a determined time, witnessed by the community as a whole; the new rites can go on indefinitely and be severed, (dropping out and being pushed out), perhaps never resulting in generation community recognition.

Thus young people experience few, if any marking points for change in status. Boateng (1993:110) suggests that the absence of rites of passage may contribute to the breakdown in the process of maturing and aid the disintegration of the important links between generations. He believes that 'intergenerational communication ensures a peaceful transition from youth to adulthood'.

In promoting rites of passage programmes, Warfield-Coppock (1990) advocates an organised community approach to restoring socialisation processes consistent with cultural resource knowledge adapted for modern society. In this way, rites of passage programmes encapsulate a broad context where harmonious development on a personal, communal and spiritual level can take place. In this context, rites of passage programmes fulfil an important role in bringing together families, groups and communities to facilitate the connection of spiritual values to the material world. As Dei (1999d:20) explains, 'spirituality supplies the context of meaning for society and regulates thought and behaviour of individuals in everyday life', and through this process nurtures the complex linkages of the spiritual and emotional wellbeing of individuals and families.

These programmes translate the principles enshrined within an African-centred value system through the seven principles of the Nguzo Saba (Karenga, 1977, 1997; Perkins, 1985), or the cardinal virtues enshrined in *Maat*, which both encapsulate the cultural foundations of African social thought.

African-centred worldviews have been articulated within the programme through the seven principles forming the value system known as the Nguzo Saba (see Table 5.1 and Karenga,1977; Perkins, 1985; Karenga, 1997).

Table 5.1   The Nguzo Saba

Principle	*Description*
Umoja (unity	To strive for and maintain unity in the family, community and nation.
Kujichagulia (self-determination)	To define ourselves, name ourselves, create for ourselves and speak for ourselves
Ujima (collective work and responsibility)	To build and maintain our community together, we must see our brothers' and sisters' problems as our problems and solve them together.
Ujamaa (co-operative economics)	Mutual financial interdependence; shared resources; balance.
Nia (purpose)	To make our collective vocation the building and eveloping of our community and to be in harmony with our spiritual purpose.
Kuumba (creativity)	To do always as much as we can, however we can, in order to leave our community more beautiful than we inherited it.
Imani (faith)	To believe with all our hearts in our parents, our teachers and our people.

Source: Based on Karenga (1997).

Many professionals in the field have utilised African-centred theories in developing frameworks for social work practice in Britain and the USA. For example, P. Hill, (1998) has produced *The Journey, an adolescent rites of passage* workbook. This programme implements the *Nguzo Saba* through various interventions and techniques. A snapshot of the programme's overall objectives offers the following points;

- learn about family, community and culture and develop skills that promote unity and interdependence
- learn about self and develop goal setting as related to personal planning
- understand the role of working with others in the community to promote collective problem-solving
- explore and demonstrate knowledge of the concepts of economics, individualism, interdependence and co-operation
- demonstrating both personal and collective community pride
- plan and complete projects that benefit the community
- define, explore, understand and affirm the value/belief systems necessary for becoming an adult

Each principle of the *Nguzo Saba* provides the focus for programme objectives and activities: for example, *Umoja* (unity) – to strive for and maintain unity in the family, community, nation and culture – activities may include creating a family tree; interviewing an elder; making a family chart with concentric circles representing various generations showing the child in the family; drawing a chart of the communities to which you belong (church, Saturday school, and so on); exploring resources that strengthen unity in families and communities.

Rites of passage programmes have tended to concentrate on the growth and development needs of young people. However, Glynn (1998) has developed a fatherhood prison programme that seeks to empower black men and their parenting role through the use of drama, the written and spoken word and movement. Glynn (1998:3) likens the process of exploring the life journey that each individual has taken to a journey of transformation. He believes that 'unless we recognise the need to redefine ourselves, and become liberated within, our souls will die'. The journey of transformation proposes to harness the potential for fathers to create, devise, and produce a way of being through a strong, vibrant and potent creative spirit that liberates the mind and taps into abilities.

In this discussion, I am mindful that there are many innovative social work models implemented by individuals, groups and organisations throughout Britain and elsewhere. There is an urgent need to document and articulate these important contributions to the social, psychological, material and spiritual wellbeing of black communities.

Although there has been limited attention given to rites of passage programmes in social work, there is research evidence available to suggest that these programmes do indeed serve the growth needs of young people and their families and communities. Wilcox (1998) researched the perspectives and experiences of eight leaders within the rites of passage movement in the USA. She identified the characteristics and essential components of these programmes. These components included knowledge systems of Africa and perceived the spiritual dimension of human beings as a key constituent in facilitating intergenerational unity and supporting the emotional and psychological wellbeing of young people.

Reaching out to black communities

Social welfare interventions by black people in their communities are important examples of practical solutions exercised in response to social need. It is within this context that cultural heritage and ways of knowing become critical for the survival and wellbeing of black people and their communities. This approach embraces the importance of locally produced knowledge emanating from cultural histories, philosophies, social interactions and experiences of daily life (Dei, 1999). These instruments provide a site where people can shape their own accounts of what is happening and what they can do to resolve any difficulties they face. This approach recognises more than just the importance of cultural background but also seeks to ascertain the various ways in which cultural resource knowledge can be utilised as a means of empowerment. In this way, community-defined aspirations become the focal priority at the grass roots level. These aspirations are reflected in the qualities of determination and vision that have sustained black communities over time. Thus marginalised groups can then be viewed as subjects of their own experiences and histories and, in this way, start to shift away from victimisation in order 'to generate relevant knowledge for collective resuscitation, spiritual rebirth and cultural renewal' (Dei, 1999c:23). The affirmation of cultural knowledge can be empowering and assist in social transformation to enable people to break away from dominant ideologies that have shaped and defined their social realities. Sudbury (1997) draws attention to the depiction of black peoples as passive victims in sociological studies which tend to provide statistical evidence of disadvantage. These studies fail to address the influence of struggles for equality and social justice located within black communities. As S. Small (1994:76) cited in Sudbury (1997), recounts:

> *Most books and reports end after they have presented an 'objective' or 'comprehensive' portrayal of the 'facts'. But this is only half the picture. We cannot stop at simply describing the facts of inequality, as if facts and processes go unchallenged; we must also compare these facts with the spirit of striving against inequality and injustice.*

These dominant ideologies are embedded in the belief structure of social work. Weick (1987) suggests that the overlay of culture expressed in the socialisation of the individual functions to create a homogeneous view of the world. Therefore, the space and capacity of people to develop within their own cultural reality is often denied. This is because the shared views about the nature of reality are invariably built upon the definition of others. Black-led organisations and social movements have drawn attention to the imposition of reality on subjugated communities by dominant groups located in the dynamics of power relationships. Foucault (1977:175) observed that 'power and knowledge directly imply one another' and are inextricably linked in the process of knowledge production and dissemination.

These observations are relevant in this discussion because it is the power 'to define reality and to have other people respond to your definition as if it were their own' which denies the consciousness of agency and serves to allow subjugated communities to be involved in their own oppression (Nobles, 1985:106). As Hardiman and Jackson (1997), cited in John (1999), maintain, this process targets a group's culture, language and history, which is often misrepresented, discounted or eradicated, and the dominant group's culture is then imposed.

Under these circumstances, to create a new definition of oneself against the background of aspersion and disparagement is a radical act. This radical act is expressed in a common thread of collective consciousness defined in the knowledge that the definitions of others could be challenged. It is through these insights that the complacency of conventional social work knowledge can be dislodged to expose hidden sources of cultural oppression. Moreover, this approach invites a dogged refusal to be intimidated by existing paradigms in forging new definitions and social realities.

Conclusion

This chapter has examined and explored existing models of social work recognised as the way forward for interventions with black families and communities. Both anti-discriminatory and ethnic-sensitive models of social work reveal several flaws that either contribute to the establishment of Eurocentric ways of knowing in social work as the norm or locate black people solely within the frame of reference of racism and oppression. In this way, the wider society has sought to institutionalise the impression that there is a societal consensus which supports universal conceptual frameworks (Stanfield, 1994). For the most part, the diverse interpretations and constructions of reality of black communities are marginalised or excluded. This means that black communities have limited choices of interpretative frameworks that are empowering and meaningful in which to enjoy and benefit from.

The strengths model of black families has been utilised in social work theory in framing empowerment models for practice. Whilst the strengths models emerged in response to the propensity of social science literature towards a dysfunctional view of balck families and sought to redress these distortions and mis-representations, the strengths model raises several problematics. How do you prove strengths in oppression without diluting and drawing attention away from the dehumanising effects of racism? Moreover, the strengths school may have unwittingly created its own negatives by suppressing the 'pathological consequences of oppression (Karenga, 1993). Surely, black families have weaknessess as well as strengths and these concerns invite questions about the ways in which a balanced appraisal can take place. One of the constant questions that emerge from these dilemmas, is how to create a 'cognitive road map' that is not only more culturally relevant but is reflective of the plural character of a British multicultural society.

This discussion raises important questions about the ways in which marginalised groups such as black communities 'construct their own words as modes of action in private spheres only, hidden from the eyes and ears of the dominant...no matter how people of colour define themselves, there are still the more powerful stereotypes embedded in public culture that define their status and identity within the cosmos of the dominant' (Stanfield, 1994:182).

Nevertheless, the adoption of strenghts and empowerment models in social work has created further opportunities to explore other avenues and pathways of empowerment located in black communities themselves.

Limited attention has been given to the possibilities and potentialities of cultural resource knowledge as the basis of social work theory and practice as a tool of empowerment for black families and communities. As social work moves into the postmodern era, the profession and its institutions face important challenges in breaking the stranglehold of institutional racism and discrimination. As a first step, there needs to be an opening-up of the structured silence that prevails in the disproportionate representation of black people subject to the social control aspects of social work and welfare statistics generally. Social work as a profession is committed to social justice, yet one of the barriers to realising this ideal may lie in the failure of social work to create opportunities to develop service models which are different from those that presently exist.

This discussion calls for the active involvement of social work in serving the needs of local communities where opportunities to spearhead new approaches to bring about racial equality, social justice and social change can be created. These considerations require meaningful partnerships with groups and organisations to be created. Community organisations can be viewed as partners and their perspectives on serving communities should be deemed legitimate by professionals. Similarly, there is a need to promote models of service delivery, which assist and strengthen community building. Building from these strengths requires the recognition and validation of skills and capacities that are often unnoticed in black-led community organisations, and an understanding of how social conditions have been improved through the active involvement of community networks.

In order for social work to contribute to the empowerment of communities, there is a need to recognise and acknowledge time-honoured institutions that have sustained communities over time. Social work has an important role to play in learning from the talents and skills within black communities themselves in order to support their self-help efforts. Cultural resource knowledge is an important tool of empowerment for black families, groups and organisations. These models of empowerment are embedded within African-centred social work. The influence of critical social theory and progressive approaches in social work can help to forge a path through which non-traditional models such as African-centred theories can assist in meeting the needs and challenges of social welfare in black communities.

Chapter 6
Exploring cultural knowledge as a source of empowerment

Social work has a long-standing association with community work. Indeed, community work has been recognised as a method of social work intervention alongside groupwork and casework (Popple, 1995). Although social work has been guided largely by a focus upon improving social functioning with individuals and families, the interface of social environments continues to shape and define approaches to practice. The person in the environment approach recognises the influence of the social environment on the wellbeing of individuals and families and the interdependence of social relationships in communities. In this respect, although social environments are often saddled with stress-inducing capacities, communities also function to provide opportunities and resources for survival, recreation and other life-sustaining patterns of human need. Communities also contain 'naturally occurring resources in the social environment' in matching individual strengths to create opportunities and initiatives in an integrated fashion (Sullivan, 1992:148).

For black communities living in the diaspora, environmental pressures (both structural and interpersonal) conspire to suppress cultural orientations within their life worlds. The consequences of oppression generate stressors such as inadequate family incomes, ill health, restricted educational opportunities, job discrimination, adverse housing conditions, and suppression of economic and community development. The material, economic and social outcomes of oppression provide a matrix in which complex forms of oppression affect both sociological and psychological dimensions. It is important to understand these complexities in order to identify the ways in which existing social work models of practice have created and contributed to conditions of oppression. The consequences should be a broader understanding of quality of life, social environments and human needs. Common definitions of social work focus upon the person and the environment. This duality and the interactions between them constitute the domain of practice that serves as a distinctive set of attributes which separates social work from other helping professions.

Person and the environment - individual and collective meanings

The systems approach in social work reflects a shift away from identifying pathology in individuals and families and towards an emphasis upon environmental problems and needs. From this perspective, the source of problems and unmet needs is located in the interactions and interface between people and their environments. In this way, the importance of the environment is secured in social work designs for practice. The systems approach draws upon general systems theory in translating its principles as conceptual tools for social work practice. The commonly cited social work concept of a person in the environment directs attention to the interrelatedness and interdependency that can be understood as an open system. Thus, 'a change in the system effects the environment and vice versa' (Stein, 1974:31). This pathway has been conceptualised as possessing three basic systems in planning and implementing service delivery: first, natural-helping systems such as informal support networks; second, formal systems such as community organisations; and third, societal systems such as institutional structures.

Davies (1977) outlines several key characteristics encompassed within the systems approach to social work.

1. The systems theory directs sources of social problems away from individual and family pathology towards an emphasis upon contemporary environments.

2. Systems theory recognises multiple factors implied in the interactions of people and society. In this context, systems theory seeks to explain and organise the complexity of dynamic interacting variables.

3. Systems theory helps social workers to consider multiple factors in an equal manner relating to the design and implementation of interventions.

4. The systems approach to social work is compatible with social work concepts and values and can therefore, be applied to group-work and community work. Moreover this approach accords with techniques found in casework theory and practice and in so doing, facilitates the use of several techniques that can be employed in the light of specific objectives. This perspective supports social work beliefs in the capacity of individuals for growth and development. In this way, the creative process in social work can generate new insights to assist individuals to seek alternative solutions to difficulties and problems.

Systems theory, then has been considered as the principal pathway to a holistic conception of social work practice (Stein, 1974). A more holistic conception of social work practice fosters dissolution of the compartmentalisation that characterises traditional casework methods. Systems theory has had pride of place in social work during the 1970s and 1980s, taking on 'a context, a rationale, a way of thinking, an operational style' in practice (Stein, 1974:35).

Within this context, people and their life worlds are viewed as systems and dysfunction arises from person-in-the-environment relationships. In this way, people are involved in a constant process of adaptation with various aspects of their environment. Indeed, Germain and Gitterman (1980:10) see the main aim of social work as being to 'strengthen the adaptive capacities of people and to influence their environments so that transactions are more adaptive'.

Recent models of systems approaches in social work place emphasis upon adaptive processes which, as Payne (1991:151) observes, 'may lead to assumptions that individuals should adapt to environments rather than vice versa'. Although the systems approach to social work provides useful insights into the interactions between individuals and environments, this approach fails to account for oppression and the realities of power (Wakefield, 1996). The process of adaptation to the environment that is implied within some aspects of this model raises important concerns. Whilst environmental change is considered, the emphasis upon adaptation on the part of the individual can serve to exacerbate oppressive practices and further subjugate black communities. This is because the process of adaptation may operate to foster behaviours in a manner that fulfils the expectations of oppressive systems (John, 1999). Moreover, as John (1999) observes:

a powerful and corrosive element of post-war British culture into which generations of Black Britishers have been and are being socialised is a culture of racism, a culture of racism which manifestly encompasses the racialisation of immigration, underachievement, school exclusions, youth unemployment ... the list is lengthy.

Hardiman and Jackson (1997), cited in John (1999:14), provide important insights into these dimensions of oppression. They maintain that 'oppression is not simply an ideology or set of beliefs that assert one group's superiority over another, nor is it random violence, harassment or discrimination toward members of target groups. A condition of oppression exists when the following key elements are in place'.

- The power to define and name reality and determine what is normal, real or correct is embedded within the agent group

- Discrimination, marginalisation and forms of differential treatment are institutionalised and systematic. These acts operate within systems as part of 'business as usual' that require no conscious efforts by individuals as they are embedded in social structures over time.

- The psychological colonisation of the subjugated group operates through socialising the group to internalise their oppressed condition and collude with an oppressive social system referred to as 'playing host to the oppressor'.

The last element accords with Freire's (1970) exposition, *Pedagogy of the Oppressed*, in which he suggests that subjugated communities sometimes internalise the ways they have been defined by majority communities. Freire (1981:151) uses the term 'cultural invasion' to describe the various forms of devaluation of identities by more socially powerful groups. In order for these strategies to succeed 'it is essential that those invaded become convinced of their intrinsic inferiority. Since everything has its opposite, if those who are invaded consider themselves inferior, they must necessarily recognise the superiority of the invaders' (cited in Cummins, 1996:12).

Historically, black communities have actively resisted 'cultural invasion' and devaluation of their humanity. This means of resistance has been referred to as 'staying power' (Fryer, 1984). According to Freire (1981,) capacities for critical thinking emerge when subjugated groups become more aware of the sources of their oppression. Freire (1981) uses the term 'conscientiza- tion' to describe the process of awareness and development of the capacity to engage in critical thinking about social conditions, exclusion, the wider society and oneself. The process of conscientisation is more than an intellec- tual exercise because it embraces social action. These action orientations towards knowledge and social transformation lead to reflection and further social action along a path of increasing liberation. Freire (1981) presents a critique of the artificial separation of theory and practice in Western education contexts. He believes that theory, reflection and action are interre- lated and part of a complete process. This complete process he refers to as praxis, which embraces both theory and social action to spearhead the growth of social awareness in repudiation of oppressive tendencies located in the mapping of reality through Western constructs. In this way, the processes of empowerment can lead to subjugated groups becoming self-conscious agents and subjects of their histories, cultures and life worlds. Freire's (1981) liberating approach to education and social action has been influential in the field of education and social development. Although his exposition gives a somewhat universal understanding of power relationships devoid of the complex processes through which race and gender hierarchies are produced and sustained, Freire's approach provides useful insights into the process of social transformation and empowerment.

Black communities as sites of resistance, solidarity and cultural empowerment

Definitions of community and the multiplicity of meanings the term invites continue to be an evolving debate and often contested terrain. This is evident in the plethora of social work literature evoking the domain of community as the main focus of discussion. Community care, community partnerships and community mental health highlight the ways in which 'community' is often raised, often without reference to its meaning and underlying allegiances towards particular political and social interests. In all areas of social work perceived needs of local communities are at the centre of devising and shaping social work delivery systems.

In recent years, feminist and black social movements have given rise to expanded notions of community, providing spaces where identities are nurtured and expressed in various forms. Although definitions of community are often loosely defined, the notion of community is generally perceived as defined geographical spaces, neighbourhoods, or social interactions and common interests.

Akbar *et al.* (1996:163) provide a useful understanding of community that transcends what is generally recognised as 'community'. First, community can be referred to as 'the interrelationship among people on the basis of shared ideas, concepts, ideology and systems of organising knowledge'. In other words, Akbar *et al.* (1996) contend that people may not live in the same neighbourhood but they have common interests, bonds of affinity and concerns tied to knowledge systems that unite their life worlds. Moreover, these shared values and ideals reveal a spiritual dimension to embrace definitions of community. In this way, moral ideals structure communities and are capable of over-riding the influence of both the physical and intellectual understandings of community. The spiritual dimension of community is often missed in understanding community functioning. Akbar *et al.* (1996:167) consider that:

> *as the mental community transcends physical boundaries, the spiritual community should help the person transcend boundaries of ideas and concepts. It should open the person to the highest expression of him/herself; it should be the basis for reconciling any discord that may occur in either of the other two communities.*

Dei (1999d) draws attention to various tensions, struggles and contradictions which are articulated within these conceptions of community. However, the integrity of community is maintained. These conceptions of community are important in the light of many critiques of the notion of a black community as meaningless and redundant. Black communities operate as an important site of resistance and as a forum of discussion, social action and social change. It would be a mistake to view these notions of community as static entities, on the contrary, communities embrace growth and development within the context of social and political times.

These understandings of community are particularly important because they invite useful insights as to why people come together. Black community activism has a long-standing history in Britain, emerging from the experiences of enslavement and deep-seated racism in Britain. Community activism has been pivotal in advocating black rights, social action and the struggle for a just society. These struggles have involved social welfare activities to ensure the wellbeing and survival of black communities against the onslaught of various hostilities.

S. Small (1994:42) refers to the determination and resilience of black communities in 'not passively [accepting] racialised hostility which bombards them; communities and cultures of resistance have been forged to oppose and overturn such hostility'. These experiences have provided the impetus for black communities to reach 'deep into their culture, religion, heritage and personal experiences to employ various tactics and strategies' of resistance (Small, 1994:13).

In this context, Beckles (1998:55) highlights the importance of black bookshops as 'a cultural and political centre'. These bookshops provide an important resource for black communities. During the 1970s and 1980s they became advice and action centres, providing access to 'suppressed' knowledges in the form of books and other materials. Parents, groups and organisations were compelled to counter the prevailing stereotypical representations of 'blackness' found in England's education and media structures: the 'Golliwog', the English Black minstrel icon found on jam jars, schoolbooks, and commercial items across the nation; the primitive or bare-breasted Black women; and the simultaneous invisibility of a multifaceted Black history, (J. Huntley, personal communication, 1994 cited in Beckles, 1998:55).

Books, magazines and newspapers have provided the vehicle where writing 'black' is expressed in various forms. This is where a written expression of experiences and theorising about the concerns and issues within black communities take place. These concerns are often located in the need to analyse social conditions and experiences of living and the dynamics of discrimination. For example, magazines such as the *Alarm* and, more recently, *Afrikan Business* and *Culture* have provided an important means of institutionalising cultural values and visions of black people, social exchanges, and mobilising communities in campaigns for social justice. In addition, these magazines and newspapers offer opportunities to network for the exchange of goods and services. These magazines and newspapers discuss the 'undiscussed' and seek to break with dominant ideologies and the falsehoods proffered about black people in the wider society; they present new understandings drawing upon the spectrum of views and concerns across black communities. Literature generated within the communities themselves theorises about the ways in which their communities have been historically disempowered in their interactions with societal institutions. Moreover, black-led community organisations and groups give space and voice to cultural values and knowledge, forging a way out of colonial mentalities and reaffirming a pride in cultural heritage. This understanding and effort to acquire, strengthen and increase cultural resource knowledge invites opportunities to incorporate these ways of knowing and living at an interpersonal level. Black-led community organisations, families and groups make important contributions in various ways to the visions and possibilities because they are community-defined aspirations given focal priority at a grass roots level. As Freire (1987:13) maintains,

> *as conscious human beings, we can discover how we are conditioned by the dominant ideology. We can gain distance on our moment of existence. Therefore, we can learn how to become free through a political struggle in society. We can struggle to become free precisely because we can know we are not free! That is why we can think of transformation.*

This space also provides the site where critical discussions and debate take place about normative beliefs and ways of knowing as people search for models of human excellence and human possibilities in the context of liberation practices. For example, in recent years many groups and organisations have been engaged in discussions about the contribution of women to black organisations and the sexism in various forms that has sought to divide black men and women. Organisations such as Kemetic Educational Guidance, the Alkebulan Revivalist Movement and others have openly sought to bring women into the centre of activities and organising. African-centred knowledge systems and efforts to incorporate the philosophy of *Maat* into day to day living and social and organisational practices have assisted in the elevation of womanhood and the unique contribution of black women to struggle, resistance and activism, and the wellbeing of communities.

It is within this context that education has particular meanings for black communities. Schooling represents one aspect of education where a particular form of engagement with dominant cultural groups in society take place (Giroux, 1985). Education transcends notions of schooling to embrace meanings, values and struggle in the context of power relationships. Education implies the process of gaining knowledge and through and along this path: the 'consciousness of knowledge allows subjects to define and determine the understanding of their own realities' (Dei, 1999b:15). In other words, the 'very act of knowing is related to the power of self-definition' (Mohanty, 1990:184, cited in Dei, 1999b:15). In this context, education can provide a critical understanding of the sources of oppression. Moreover, through cultural resource knowledge linkages are made between social theory and practice to the deepest aspects of emancipation in order to humanise life. This is the site where individuals and groups fashion possibilities, meaning, desires and struggles about futures and a particular way of life.

Education as a referent for social change gives rise to an understanding that knowledge can be used to challenge and resist strategies of domination in knowledge production and dissemination. Education defined in this way invites a refutation of the historical disparagement of black people as intellectually inferior and gives rise to an understanding of the ways in which forms of oppression come together to actively silence subjugated groups from knowledge production and dissemination. Education has become a driving force for the success of individuals and communities (Mirza and Reay, 2000).

From this perspective, cultural resource knowledge provides a vehicle for the intellectual, emotional, physical and spiritual wellbeing of individual and communities in pursuit of educational transformation. This expanded understanding of education gives voice and opportunity to the various strategies and choices and ways through which people come to know their life worlds and are active within various spaces (Dei, 1999c). In this way, black communities engage in strategies through, and social action orientated approaches in, striving for models of success. Social welfare activities in black communities invite opportunities for people to become self-conscious agents, creating strategies of empowerment and empowering each other through social action orientated programmes, study groups and meetings at a grass roots level. These forms of action emerge 'from a joining of the languages of critique and possibility' inspiring visions of futures (Giroux, 1985:xiii). This is where people construct spaces to move beyond survival and strive towards success by any means necessary.

For example, Mirza and Reay (2000:523) argue that black supplementary schools are more than a response to poor educational provision and mainstream educational exclusion. They have developed as 'a covert movement for social change' and social transformation. Communities are created through collective agency, reciprocity and continuity (Mirza and Reay, 2000).

Mirza and Reay's (2000) research study of black supplementary schools highlights the dedication and commitment of black mothers in organising supplementary schools, creating and sustaining social networks in order to provide resources from black communities themselves. The authors maintain that:

> *black supplementary schools paradoxically embody elements of both masculine individualism and feminine co-operation. Within a wider social context in which British consciousness, whether black or white, is currently preoccupied with individualism, black supplementary schools are simultaneously places of collectivity at the same time* (Mirza and Reay, 2000;531)

These understandings accord with African-centred ways of knowing in seeking balance and mutuality in social relationships. Mirza and Reay's (2000) discussions attempt to present a black women's feminist discourse that dislodges black male involvement and contributions. Whilst it can be argued that social welfare activities within black-led community organisations have been the principal domain of women, recent developments indicate that this is changing as coalitions are being created and sustained between women and men.

Sudbury (1997:193) draws attention to the acknowledgement by many black men involved in community activism of the 'gendered experiences of racism and community'. She suggests for the first time, 'it is black men who are exploring problems within black communities and the impact of racism in reinforcing these problems'.

The contribution of black women to the education of children in black communities and as bearers of culture accords with the research of Dove (1998). Dove's thesis provides an account of black women's attempts to challenge and resist contemporary conditions in relation to schooling and education. These herstories speak of their cultural memory and knowledge handed down to their children in black supplementary schools. From an black womanist perspective, black supplementary schools provide a space where cultural knowledge can be disseminated and become a driving force in social transformation and social change. These spaces of collective action are where 'black women work to keep alive the black communities' collective desire for self-knowledge' (Mirza and Reay, 2000:539).

Although Mirza and Reay (2000) claim that the mission of black supplementary schools participating in their research embraced an integration of educational success while 'remaining true to their origins', the importance and role of cultural resource knowledge is limited to subjective black experiences.

The relegation of cultural resource knowledge to the periphery of their analysis highlights a missed opportunity in uncovering the manner in which ways of knowing through cultural resource knowledge provide an anchor and informs discourses of blackness, its patterns and forms of empowerment. Uncovering hidden subjugated knowledges entails more than black perspectives and experiences: these endeavours require understanding of the ways in which black communities search deep into cultural heritage to empower and bring to the fore possibilities and potentialities in striving to create human excellence and futures.

Christian (1998) clarifies the concept of empowerment as exemplified in the grassroots of black communities. He argues that black communities in Liverpool with a long history of settlement are in dire need of empowerment initiatives. Empowerment from this perspective is directed by social welfare interests from the cultural base of black communities as well as from a 'black community position'. According to Christian (1998), empowerment initiatives must be more than giving 'voice to the voiceless' and should enhance black efforts to secure self-help programmes. Empowerment in black communities requires meaningful community-based strategies. This approach embraces a 'seeing is believing' perspective where:

> *an individual from any social background can become whatever he or she wants to be provided they have the energy and commitment to reach where they want to be in the given society. Moreover, if a community organisation does not reflect the broader society's population in terms of its staff at all the various levels of hierarchy and/or power positions, then it should be deemed as an organisation that is not offering empowerment in practice.* (Christian, 1998:24)

Black-led efforts for change in social work

> *There is no single area of our lives, which better exposes our experience of institutional racism than our relationship with various welfare agencies.* (Bryan et al., 1985:110)

Over the past decades, some black people and activists have regarded social work as the 'bane' of black communities. The perception of the profession as a social enforcement agency is borne out in the over representation of black people subject to the social control aspects of social work. The sustained over-representation of black children in the care system has been a particular area of controversy, disquiet and dismay among black professionals in the field and communities alike. For example, during the 1970s, disproportionate numbers of black children found themselves drifting in the public care system along the pathway of short-term voluntary care, being placed with culturally inappropriate families away from their communities. Community activists and black professionals have drawn attention to the experiences of black families in receipt of social work services.

Penny and Best (1988:3) highlight the double-bind scenarios that many black families experienced in the 1970s and 1980s:

If they were not saying that they wished to remove their children from care; they were seen as not putting the children's needs first and not really caring for them; if they did demand the return of their children, they were told that after so many years in care they were being unreasonable and bad to think that they could reintroduce the child so easily into their families. They were told there were going to be real problems, that the child was likely to be unable or willing to accept them as full time parents; they were told to put the child's needs first and consider the disruption they would cause to their child if it was removed from the only home or family the child really knew.

In landmark studies, such as *Children Who Wait* (Rowe and Lambert, 1973), the high proportion of black children in residential care or foster care who were drifting through the system devoid of any long-term plans for their future was highlighted. These children were often perceived as 'hard to place', and therefore deemed as having little hope of experiencing family life. In Bryan *et al.*, (1985:116), black women speak of their experiences of interactions with the instruments of social welfare; they often considered 'the children's' home [as] ... a stop-over for young offenders, meaning that our experience can be a criminalising one'. According to these authors, institutional racism created a dysfunctional social welfare system that encouraged the break-up of black families, yet refused to consider black families as substitute carers.

These concerns provided the impetus for black social workers in the field and black activists to challenge and demand social change. New social workers coming into the profession in the early 1980s supported small groups of established social workers to produce an upsurge of activity that was conspicuous for several years, advocating and demanding radical change in social work practice with black families and children. These activities and challenges initiated the formation of Black Workers' Groups in many social work departments in Britain. These groups formulated strategies to challenge policy and practice and initiate new directions. The opposition to change was often advanced under the guise of questioning the 'professionalism' of black social workers. However, the determination and vision of many black social workers assisted in forcing through changes at a local level.

Many black social workers striving for change recognised the need for a nation-wide organisation to be established to effect social welfare reforms within a wider context: thus the Association of Black Social Workers and Allied Professionals was conceived. ABSWAP also consisted of social workers and professionals from various minoritised communities. ABSWAP spearheaded the campaign for the rights of black children to be placed with black families. John Small, the first president of ABSWAP, published a series of articles advocating the end of transracial placements and the need for new initiatives in black communities, starting with the recruitment of black foster carers and adopters.

ABSWAP's evidence to the House of Commons Select Committee in 1983, and high-profile campaign highlighting the plight of black children in care, played a major role in shaping the legislative framework in addressing the needs of black children and their families.

The Children Act 1989 provides a comprehensive legal framework to protect and promote the interests and welfare of children. For the first time in British child-care legislation the Act introduced a statutory obligation upon local authorities to give due consideration to racial origin, ethnic background, religion and language in the provision and delivery of services. In this way, ABSWAP played a major role in shifting the ideological base of social work practice (Prevatt, 2000). This pioneering group of black activists challenged prevailing myths and stereotypes about black families and communities, contemporaneously identifying dysfunctional elements within the general system of child-care that served to compound oppression, discrimination and undermine the integrity of black parents and communities. Many black professionals, groups and organisations brought to the fore the underlying philosophies of social services that produced over-arching models of social work delivery founded upon a 'like it or lump it attitude' implicated in assimilationist policies (Cheetham, 1981; Connelly, 1981).

Ahmad (1989:163) suggests that the concepts of assimilation and integration were based upon 'a firm belief that black children were part of the "new immigrants" and in time they would be integrated into the western way of life'. These beliefs were based upon the following precepts. First, the integration of black children into a British way of life would assist in the maintenance of harmonious race relations. Second, as black children became integrated they would adapt to the service structures already in place. This would benefit both black children and their families. Third, integration was in the best interests of black children because of the superiority of Western culture. The cultural traditions of black communities were perceived as 'inferior' and not in keeping with modern society. Fourth, the accommodation of child-care services to the needs of black children was considered to be working against assimilation and integration and hence could be viewed as discriminatory.

Within this context, the first black agency, New Black Families, was set up in 1980 to recruit black families to adopt and foster black children in the care of Lambeth Social Services. New Black Families, under the directorship of John Small, challenged deficit models of black families in social work. He explained that the unit:

has brought a new approach to family finding in the sense that its assumptions are different from more orthodox agencies. It recognises and values the experience and competence of black families as parents and child rearers and accepts the validity of different life styles and child-care practices (Small, 1982:35).

Small considers that every black child should have the opportunity to enter into a black family in the same way this opportunity has been offered to white children (Prevatt, 2000). I support Prevatt's (2000) acknowledgement that social work owes a debt to pioneering black activists and professionals in forcing through a number of changes in social work policy and practice. Local authorities and adoption services were able to learn from black organisations, churches and other religious organisations how to reach out to black communities to find substitute families.

These efforts to initiate changes in social work policy and practice produced sporadic responses in social work agencies. For example, some local authorities set up specific family placement teams with remits to tap into resources within black communities to facilitate the recruitment of foster carers and adopters. A wider understanding of family forms was acknowledged as potentially able to provide substitute care. Thus foster and adoption programmes for potential substitute carers were designed to meet the specific needs of black families. Traditional methods of assessment were rejected in favour of more culturally competent formats.

The London Borough of Lambeth produced a 'Good Practice Guide for Working with Black Families and Children'. This document was utilised by agencies and organisations in the planning and delivery of services to black communities.

Limited reforms in social work policy and practice were replicated throughout social service departments involved in family placements. Although the contentious debates about transracial placements reached their height during the 1980s, this area of child-care continues to evoke discussion in academic circles as well as social work generally. In recent times social work (and social work education in particular) has been the subject of a backlash against the progressive approaches with regard to the placement needs of black children. Barn (1999:15) maintains that:

> *the colour-blind emphasis of 'love not colour' spearheaded by the former Junior Health Minister, Paul Boateng, is misguided and short-sighted. Whilst some black youngsters experience happy and stable homes, the social and psychological problems encountered by the majority of black youngsters in transracial family settings have been documented by research in both the UK and the US. Black children in the public care system are subjected to a reality of isolation, alienation and marginalisation.*

Research undertaken by Ince (1999:161) documents the experiences of young black people in the public care system. Ince highlights the role of culture and its importance to black young people growing up in Britain. She reported that young black people often experienced a lack of contact with their family of origin and black communities. These experiences of loss and separation became a consistent feature of their lives. Thus, their life worlds were characterised by separation from black families and communities which contributed to the loss of 'meanings, values, folkways, symbols and tradition...and effectively dislocated the young people from any understanding of themselves and gave opportunity for negative value systems and confusion over racial identity to develop'. As a consequence of this process the role of culture and its meanings and value was not considered, or else it was devalued. Thus, cultural resource knowledges were perceived as unimportant and so young black people had a restricted understanding of culture on which to draw upon for methods of resistance and empowerment. Ince provides an important theoretical model that serves to identify the psychological dimensions of racism and the coping mechanisms developed by young people to deal with racism. These psychological dimensions of racism are discussed in the following way.

First, the experiences of being in care produced negative feelings and low self-esteem. Second, young black people felt alienated from their culture and 'race'. In this way due to 'the absence of positive black role models, all of the study sample reconstructed their internal worlds to idealise the people who were in many ways their oppressors by wanting to be white themselves or seeing themselves as individuals, but not black individuals' (Ince, 1999:164). These factors combined to compound a sense of dislocation and separation from the cultural and spiritual self. These dimensions of self are tied to understandings of emotional and spiritual wellbeing.

Dei (1999) suggests that it is through the affirmation of the connections between spirituality, collective consciousness and socio-political agency that spiritual knowing and human emotions become 'legitimate and intelligible' knowledge. Spiritual knowing entails the individual sharing experiences of the universal meaning of human existence through 'being in community and being in relationship to other people' (Miller, 1999:4, cited in Dei, 1999:20). In this context, spirituality supplies the context and meaning for communities. Spirituality can be experienced in the individual sense of being in connection with the collective. African-centred approaches view these aspects of self as central to harmony and wellbeing and nurture them via conceptions of personhood through and within connections with family, social networks and communities.

According to Schiele (2000), one of the critical consequences of oppression is spiritual alienation. This particular outcome of oppression is often given limited attention. While it is important to explore and address the political, social and economic consequences of oppression, African-centred perspectives seek to uncover multidimensional understandings of oppression, as a source of social problems. These understandings of the outcomes of oppression in its various forms and guises foster spiritual alienation and separation of the spiritual and material realms of life. These contingencies restrict human growth and potential. Spiritual wellness, on the other hand, is defined as 'openness to the spiritual dimensions that permits the integration of one's spirituality with the other dimensions of life, thus maximising the potential for growth and self-actualisation' (Westgate, 1996:27, cited in Schiele, 2000:66).

Towards new approaches to empowering black communities
Although black families and children are often recipients of social work interventions, social work has not adequately explored ways of working that foster greater equality directed towards social change. One of the consistent themes of this book has been a focus upon prevailing ethnocentric perspectives with some modification and adaptation as the way forward in addressing the needs of black families and communities. These perspectives

are found in conventional social work methods that consider 'either explicitly or implicitly the norms, values, or needs of the majority culture to be the most desirable' (Gutierrez and Nagda, 1996:204).

Social work as a profession in Britain has been subject to important changes in working practices largely through legislative frameworks, as well as occupational fragmentation over the past decades. These changes reflect the current socio-political and economic environment that has always influenced the goals, priorities and methodologies of the social work profession. Social work has been firmly placed within a remit of responsive actions on an individual and family basis to social problems and difficulties. The preventative aspects of social work usually found in community approaches are usually relegated to the periphery in the planning of community services to tackle the social inequalities apparent in British society.

Some commentators in recent years have suggested that social work has abandoned its mission to assist oppressed communities (Specht and Courtney, 1994). Social work as a profession has often adopted an individualised understanding of empowerment located in exclusive notions of user involvement in services already established.

This discussion begs the question of what kind of services would be available and what would be their principal constituents if social work embraced its core value of social justice in shaping the contours of service provision and interventions (Gutierrez and Nagda, 1996). This is one of the challenges facing social work and can be explored and addressed in the following ways.

First, social work is ideally placed to create a dual focus in forcing through social change to provide empowering programmes and services to black communities. This requires the creation of critical alliances with black communities. A first step could be improved recognition of the valuable contribution which black-led organisations, black churches and other religious organisations have made in improving the social conditions of black communities through the involvement of community networks, together with an acknowledgement of the importance of empowerment through organisational autonomy. This assertion may seem contrary to my arguments about cultural inclusion; however, as I have mentioned in previous chapters, African-centred approaches to social welfare support and value spaces where black people can re-affirm cultural values and gain power through identifying and theorising about sources of oppression through critical consciousness. Moreover, this space opens up avenues and pathways where black communities can build and establish cultural institutions. Furthermore this is an area where cultural pluralism can be nurtured and fully realised to the benefit of society as a whole.

Second, commitment to an empowerment perspective in social work requires not only respect for and understanding of cultural resource knowledges but seeks to uncover and utilise cultural knowledge as a source and means of empowerment.

Third, an empowerment perspective in social work builds close links and alliances with black communities, including an array of social networks. This perspective recognises and acknowledges time-honoured institutions that have sustained communities over time. Social work seeks to learn from the talents and skills within black communities themselves in order to support their self-help efforts. Organisations and agencies that work together and create partnerships and alliances can provide better and more appropriate services.

The notion of partnerships has become central to principles of participatory practice. Partnerships can take various forms across the field of social work. Partnerships in the context of black communities require focus upon community strengths and capacities, and the recognition and validation of knowledge and skills as an integral constituent of how best to ensure community involvement in the regeneration of communities. These considerations are important because partnerships inevitably imply a degree of equity between partners, yet partnerships are affected by power relationships in wider society. Social work over time has developed skills in effective partnerships with families and other professionals. These strengths and capacities can be usefully employed in creating meaningful partnerships with black communities.

Conclusion

This chapter has discussed various forms of empowerment located in cultural 'spaces' in black communities. Historically, black communities have often perceived social work in a negative light. Community activists have drawn attention to the oppressive aspects of social work interventions that have resulted in conflict and controversy. These contentious issues are often found in social work's role as agents of social control. It appears that authorities have very little regard to the dynamics of racism and the marginalisation of black people. This is evident in the nature of social work operating within state institutions where the profession is shaped by the very system it is attempting to change. It is within this context that African-centred social work can assist in breaking down intellectual arrogance 'about the certainty of knowledge that pretends to know and understand all forms of oppression' (Dei,1999b:21).

Black-led efforts to spearhead changes in social work policy and practice brought into sharp focus the concerns and perspectives of black communities and black professionals in the field. Cultural histories, experiences and position in society informed their perspectives and definitions of social work. Community-based understanding of social work embraces contextual and cultural knowledge in serving the needs of local communities. Community engagement invites and links social work to the realities of oppression. Black communities are deliberating upon areas of their lives which are marginalised by society. They are formulating their own agendas at local levels to address their needs and concerns.

Black communities, through social welfare activities and study groups, are engaged in revitalising past traditions, histories and cultures which have historically been disparaged by the wider society. In codifying these cultural values, explanations of human behaviour and empowerment can be realised through a more culturally-centred approach to reality.

Social work has held conceptions of social justice and equality at the heart of the profession. It is now time for these ideals to be realised through the validation of intellectual endeavours, social realities and lived experiences across the multiplicity of human knowledge. In this way, social work ensures its participation in creating conditions for cultural inclusion that reflects Britain's multicultural society.

References

Abarry, A (1990) 'Afrocentricity: Introduction', *Journal of Black Studies*, 21, pp 123–5.

ABSWAP (1983) *Black Children in Care - Evidence to the House of Commons Social Services Committee* London, ABSWAP.

Adam, B D (1978) *The Survival of Domination: inferiorization and everyday life* New York, Elsevier.

Ahmad, B (1990) *Black Perspectives in Social Work* Birmingham, Venture Press.

Ahmad, B (1989) 'Childcare and ethnic minorities' in Kahan, B (ed.) *Child Care Research, Policy and Practice* London, Hodder & Stoughton and Open University.

Akbar, N (1976) 'Rhythmic patterns in African personality' in King, L and Dixon V, and Nobles W (eds) *African Philosophy: assumptions and paradigms for research on black people* Los Angeles, CA, Fanon Research Development Center.

Akbar, N (1984) 'Afrocentric social sciences for human liberation' *Journal of Black Studies* 14(4), 395–414.

Akbar, N (1985) 'Our destiny: Authors of a scientific revolution' in McAdoo, H, and McAdoo, J (eds) *Black Children: social psychological and educational environments* Beverley Hills, CA, Sage .

Akbar, N, Saafir, R and Granberry, D (1996) 'Community psychology and systems intervention' in Azibo ya Ajani Daudi, (ed.) *African Psychology in Historical Perspective and Related Commentary* Trenton, NJ, Africa World Press.

Allen, P (1992) T*he Sacred Hoop, Recovering the Feminine in American Indian Traditions* Boston, MA, Beacon Press.

Alleyne, M (1971) 'The linguistic continuity of African in the Caribbean' in Richards, H (ed.) *Topics in Afro-American Studies* Buffalo, Black Academy Press.

Anderson, M L (1993) 'Studying across difference: Race, class, and gender in qualitative research' in Stanfield, J H and Dennis, R M (eds) *Race and Ethnicity in Research Methods* Newbury Park, CA, Sage.

Ani, M (1994) *Yurugu – an African-centred critique of European thought and behaviour* Trenton,. NJ, Africa World Press.

Arewa, C S (1998) *Opening to Spirit: Contacting the Healing Power of the Chakras and Honouring African Spirituality* London, Thorsons.

Asante, M (1980) 'International/intercultural relations' in Asante, M and Vandi, A (eds) *Contemporary Black Thought: Alternative analyses in social and behavioural science* Beverley Hills, CA: Sage.

Asante, M (1987) *The Afrocentric Idea* Philadelphia, PA, Temple University Press.

Asante, M (1988) *Afrocentricity: The Theory of Social Change* Trenton, NJ, Africa World Press.

Asante, M (1990) *Kemet, Afrocentricity and Knowledge* Trenton, NJ, Africa World Press.

Asante, M (1994) *Malcom X as Cultural Hero and other Afrocentric Essays* Trenton, NJ, Africa World Press.

Asante, M, and Abarry, A (1995) *African Intellectual Heritage: a Book of Sources* Philadelphia, Temple University Press.

Banks, S (1995) *Ethics and Values in Social Work* London, Macmillan.

Banton, M (1972) *Racial Minorities* London, Fontana.

Barn, R (1993) *Black Children in the Public Care System* London, Batsford.

Barn, R, Sinclair, R and Ferdinand, D (1997) *Acting on Principle: an examination of race and ethnicity in social services provision for children and families* London, British Agencies for Adoption and Fostering.

Barn, R (1999) 'Racial and ethnic identity' in Barn, R (ed.) *Working with Black Children and Adolescents in Need* London, British Agencies for Adoption and Fostering.

Bar-On, A A (1994) 'The elusive boundaries of social work' *Journal of Sociology and Social Welfare* 21, pp 53–67.

Bar-On, A A (1999) 'Social work and the "missionary zeal to whip the heathen along the path of righteousness"' *British Journal of Social Work* 29, pp 5–26.

Bascom, W R (1952) 'The Esusu: A credit institution of the Yoruba' *Journal of the Royal Anthropological Institute of Great Britain* 82, 1, pp 62-70.

Bauman, Z (1991) *Modernity and Ambivalence* Cambridge, Polity Press.

Beattie, J (1770) *An Essay on the Nature and Immutability of Truth in Opposition to Sophistry and Scepticism* Philadelphia, PA, Solomon Wieatt, 1809.

Beckles, C (1998) 'We shall not be terrorised out of existence, the political legacy of England's black bookshops' *Journal of Black Studies* 29(1), pp 51-72.

Belenky, M F, Clinchy, B, Goldberger, N and Tarule, J (1986) *Women's Ways of Knowing* New York, Basic Books.

References

Bernal, M (1987) *Black Athena* London, Free Association Press.

Bernard, J (1973) 'My four revolutions: An autobiographical history of the American Sociological Society' *American Journal of Sociology* 78, pp 773–91.

Bewaji, J (1995) 'Critical comments on Pearce, African Philosophy and the Sociological Thesis' *Philosophy of the Social Sciences* 25(1), pp 99–119.

Biestek, F (1961) *The Casework Relationship* London, Allen & Unwin.

Billingsley, A (1968) *Black Families in White America* Englewood Cliffs, NJ, Prentice-Hall.

Billingsley, A and Giovannoni, J (1972) *Children of the Storm* New York, Harcourt Brace Jovanovich.

Boateng, F (1993) 'African traditional education: a tool for intergenerational communication' in Asante, M K and Asante, K W (eds) *African Culture The Rhythms of Unity* Trenton, NJ, Africa World Press.

Bolt, C (1971) *Victorian Attitudes to Race* London, Routledge Kegan & Paul.

Boneparth, E (1978) 'Evaluating women's studies: academic theory and practice' in Blumhagen, K O and Johnson, W D (eds) *Women's Studies: contributions in women's studies* Westport, CT, Greenwood.

Bordo, S (1990) 'Feminism, postmodernism and gender scepticism' in Nicholson, L, (ed) *Feminism/Postmodernism* London, Routledge.

Bowpitt, G (1998) 'Evangelical Christianity, secular humanism, and the genesis of British social work' *British Journal of Social Work* 28(5) pp 675–93.

Braidwood, S (1994) *London's Black Poor and the foundation of the Sierra Leone Settlement 1786-1791* Liverpool, Liverpool University Press.

Bristow, A R and Esper, J A (1988) 'A feminist research ethos' in Nebraska Sociological Feminist Collective, *A Feminist Ethic for Social Science Research* Lewiston, NY, The Edwin Mellen Press.

Browne, C (1995) 'Empowerment in social work practice with older women' *Social Work* 40, 3, pp 358–64.

Bryan, B, Dadzie, S and Scafe, S (1985) *The Heart of the Race, Black Women's Lives in Britain* London, Virago.

Bryan, A (1992) 'Working with black single mothers: myths and reality' in Langan, M and Day, L (eds) *Women, Oppression and Social Work* London, Routledge.

Bullis, R (1996) *Spirituality in Social Work Practice* Washington, DC, Taylor Francis.

Burman, E (1994) *Deconstructing Developmental Psychology* London, Routledge.

Burton, A (1998) 'States of injury: Josephine Butler on slavery, citizenship and the Boer war' *Social Politics* 5(3), pp 338–61.

Butler, S and Wintram, C (1991) *Feminist Groupwork* London, Sage.

Canda, E (1988) 'Conceptualising spirituality of social work: insights from diverse perspectives' *Social Thought* 13, pp 30–46.

Carlton-LaNey, I (1999) 'African American social work pioneers' response to need' *Social Work* 44(4) 311–21.

Carmichael, S and Hamilton, C (1968) *Black Power – The Politics of Liberation in America* London, Jonathan Cape.

Cashmore, E (1979) *Rastaman* London, Allen & Unwin.

Cassirer, E (1951) *The Philosophy of the Enlightenment* Princeton,NJ Princeton University Press

CCETSW (1989) *Requirements and Regulations for the Diploma in Social Work, Paper 30* London CCETSW.

Centre for Contemporary Cultural Studies, (1982) *The Empire Strikes Back: Race and Racism in 70s Britain* London, Hutchinson.

Cheetham, J (1982) *Social Work Services for Ethnic Minorities in Britain and the USA* London, Department of Health and Social Services.

Chestang, L (1974) 'The issue of race in social work' in Weinberger, P (ed.) *Perspectives in Social Welfare* New York, Macmillian.

Chissell, J T (1994) *Pyramids of Power! An Ancient African Centred Approach to Optimal Health* Baltimore, MD, Positive Perceptions.

Chrisman, R (1973) 'Aspects of Pan-Africanism' *Black Scholar* 4(10), pp 2–5.

Christian, M (1998) 'Empowerment and black communities in the UK: with special reference to Liverpool' *Community Development Journal* 33(1) pp 18–31.

Clark, C (2000) *Social Work Ethics: Politics, Principles and Practice* London, Macmillan.

Clarke, J H (1990) 'Pan-Africanism: a brief history of an idea in the African world', *Third World First* 1(12), pp 9–28

Cloke, C and Davies, M (eds) (1995) *Participation and Empowerment in Child Protection* London, Pitman.

Clough, P (1994) *Feminist Thought* Oxford, Blackwell Publishers.

References

Clough, S (1960) *Basic Values of Western Civilisation* New York, Columbia University Press.

Connelly, N (1981) *Social Services Provision in Multi-Racial Areas* London, Policy Studies Institute (PSI Research Paper 81/4).

Cress-Wesling, F (1973) 'Conversation with Frances Wesling' *Essence* (October).

Cugoano, O (1787) *Thoughts and Sentiments on the evil and wicked traffic of the slavery and commerce of the human species, humbly submitted to the inhabitants of Great-Britain* London, Dawsons of Pall Mall (reprinted 1969).

Cummins, J (1996) *Negotiating Identities: education for empowerment in a diverse society* Ontario, OISE, California Association for Bilingual Education.

Curtin, P (1965) T*he Image of Africa. British ideas and action 1780–1850* London Macmillan.

Davies, M (1977) *Support Systems in Social Work* London, Routledge & Kegan Paul.

Davidson, B (1991) *African Civilization Revisted: from antiquity to modern times* Trenton, NJ, Africa World Press.

Dei, G (1999a) 'The denial of difference: reframing anti-racist praxis' *Race, Ethnicity and Education* 2(1) pp 17–37.

Dei, G (1999b) *Recasting Anti-racism and the Axis of Difference: beyond the question of theory* Department of Sociology and Equity Studies in Education, OISE, University of Toronto, Canada.

Dei, G (1999c) *'Rethinking the role of Indigenous Knowledges in the academy'*. Public lecture, Department of Sociology and Equity Studies in Education, OISE, University of Toronto.

Dei, G (1999d) *'Why write 'Black'?: reclaiming African cultural resource knowledges in diasporic contexts* Department of Sociology and Equity Studies in Education, OISE, University of Toronto, Canada.

Denney, D (1983) 'Some Dominant Perspectives in the Literature Relating to Multi-Racial Social Work' *British Journal of Social Work* 13(2) pp149-74.

Derrida, J (1981) *Positions* Chicago, IL, University of Chicago Press.

Devore, W and Schlesinger, E G (1991) *Ethnic-sensitive Social Work Practice* New York, Macmillan.

Diallo, Y and Hall, M (1989) *The Healing Drum: African Wisdom Teachings* VT, Destiny Books.

Diop, C (1974) *The African Origin of Civilisation, Myth or Reality?* Westport, CT, Lawrence Hill.

Diop, C (1978) *The Cultural Unity of Black Africa* Chicago, IL, Third World Press.

Diop, C (1987) *Precolonial Black Africa* Westport, CT, Lawrence Hill.

Diop, C (1991) *Civilisation or Barbarism* New York, Lawrence Hill Books.

Dixon, V (1976) 'Worldviews and research methodology' in King L, Dixon, V and Nobles, W (eds) *African Philosophy: assumptions and paradigms for research on black persons* Los Angeles, Fanon Centre Publication, Charles Drew Postgraduate Medical School.

Dominelli, L (1988) *Anti-Racist Social Work* London, Macmillan.

Dominelli, L and Mcleod, E (1989) *Feminist Social Work* London, Macmillan.

Dominelli, L (1997) *Anti-Racist Social Work 2nd edn* Basingstoke, Macmillan.

Dove, N (1995) 'The emergence of black supplementary schools as forms of resistance to racism in the United Kingdom' in M J Shujaa, (ed.) *Too Much Schooling Too Little Education, A Paradox of Black Life in White Societie*s Trenton, Africa World Press.

Dove, N (1990) *Racism and its Effects on the Quality of Education and the Educational Performance of the Black Child* London, Institute of Education, University of London.

Dove, N (1998) *Afrikan Mothers, Bearers of Culture, Makers of Social Change* Albany, NY, State University of New York.

Dove, N (2000) *Understanding the status of women using a mother-centred matrix to analyse the depictions of women in different State formations* Lecture given at Centre for Diopian Inquiry for Research on education as cultural transmission.   Uncovering Connections Conference, 24 March, Brooklyn, New York.

Driver C (1982) 'West Indian Families: An anthropological perspective' in *Families in Britain* Rapport and Fogarty (eds) London, Routledge and Kegan Paul.

DuBois, W E B (1935) *Black Reconstruction: an essay toward a history of the part which black folk played in the attempt to reconstruct democracy in America, 1860–1880* Reprinted. New York: Russell & Russell, 1956

DuBois, W E B (1969) *The Negro American Family* New York, New American Library.

Early, T and GlenMaye, L (2000) 'Valuing families: social work practice with families from a strengths perspective' *Social Work* 45(2), pp 118–29.

Edwards, P and Dabydeen, D (1991) *Black Writers in Britain 1760–1890* Edinburgh, EdinburghUniversity Press.

Ellison, R (1965) *Invisible Man* Harmondsworth, Penguin.

English, P and Kalumba, K (1996) *African Philosophy, a Classical Approach* Englewood Cliffs, NJ, Prentice Hall

English, R (1974) 'Beyond pathology: research and theoretical perspectives on black families' in Gary L (ed.) *Social Research and the Black Community: Selected Issues and Priorities* Washington DC, Institute of Urban Affairs and Research, Howard University

Equiano, O (1794) *The Life of Olaudah Equiano, or Gustavus Vassa the African* reprinted London, Longman, 1988.

Everett, J., Chipungu, S. and Leashore, B (eds.) (1991) *Child Welfare: An Afrocentric perspective* New Brunswick, NJ, Rutgers University Press.

Ewalt, P and Mokuau, N (1995) 'Self-determination from a Pacific perspective' *Social Work* 40(2) pp 145–288.

Eze, E (1997) *Race and the Enlightenment* Oxford, Basil Blackwell.

Eze, E (1998) 'Modern Western philosophy and African colonialism' in Eze, E (ed.) *African Philosophy an Anthology*, Oxford, Basil Blackwell.

Fido, J (1977) 'The Charity Organisation Society and social casework in London 1869–1900' in Donajgrodzki, A (ed.) *Social Control in Nineteenth Century Britain* London, Croom Helm.

Fitzherbert, K (1967) *West Indian Children in London* London, Bell & Sons.

Foucault, M (1972) *The Archaeology of Knowledge* New York, Pantheon.

Foucault, M (1977) *Discipline and Punish* London, Allen Lane.

Foucault, M (1980) *Power/Knowledge* Brighton, Harvester Press.

Frankfort, Henri (1948) Ancient Egyptian Religion, New York, Harper Torch.

Fraser, D (1976) *The New Poor Law in the Nineteenth Century* London, Macmillan.

Freire, P (1981) *Pedagogy of the Oppressed* (first published 1970) New York, Continuum.

Freire, P and Shor, I (1987) *A Pedagogy for Liberation, Dialogues on Transforming Education* London, Macmillan.

Friedlander, W (1976) *Concepts and Methods in Social Work Practice* Englewood Cliffs, NJ, Prentice-Hall.

Frost, N and Stein, M (1989) *The Politics of Child Welfare, Inequality, Power and Change* Brighton,Harvester Wheatsheaf.

Fryer, P (1984) *Staying Power: The history of black people in Britain* London, Pluto Press.

Fu-Kiau, K, Kia & Lukondo-Wamba, A (1988) *Kindezi: The Kongo Art of Babysitting* Baltimore, MD, Imprint.

Gambrill, E (1997) 'Social work education: current concerns and possible futures' in Reish, M and Gambrill, E (eds) *Social Work in the 21st Century* Thousand Oaks, California, Pine Forge.

Garry, A and Pearsall, M (eds) (1992) *Women, Knowledge and Reality* London, Routledge.

General Evening Post, 21 February 1786 quoted in Shyllon, F (1977) 'Black People in Britain 1555–1833' London, Institute of Race Relations, Oxford University Press.

George, D M (1987) *London Life in the Eighteenth Century* Harmondsworth, Penguin.

Germain, C and Gitterman, A (1980) *A Life Model of Ssocial Work Practice* New York: Columbia University Press.

Gerzina, G (1995) *Black England: Life before emancipation* London, John Murray.

Gill O and Jackson B (1983) *Adoption and Race: black, Asian and mixed race children in white families* London, Batsford Press.

Gilligan, C (1988) *Mapping the Moral Domain: a contribution to women's thinking in psychological theory and education* Cambridge, MA, Harvard University Press.

Gilroy, P. (1993) *The Black Atlantic* London, Verso

Gilroy, P (1982) 'Police and Thieves' in Hall, S *et al.* (eds) *The Empire Strikes Back* Centre for Contemporary Cultural Studies, London, Hutchinson

Giroux, H. (1985) Introduction in Freire, P. *The Politics of Education, Culture, Power and Liberation,* Basingstoke, Macmillan

Glynn, M (1998) *Soulfires (a fatherhood prison programme)* Birmingham, England.

Goldberg, D T (1993) *Racist Culture: Philosophy and the Politics of Meaning* Oxford, Basil Blackwell.

Goldberg, D T (2000) 'Racial knowledge' in Back, L and Solomos, J (eds) *Theories of Race and Racism* London, Routledge.

Goody, J (1962) *Death, Property and the Ancestors* Stanford, CA, Stanford University Press.

Gordon, C (1980) *Power/Knowledge, Selected Interviews and Other Writings, 1972-1977* Michel Foucoult, Brighton, Harvester.

Gordon, W (1975) 'Knowledge and value: Their distinction and relationship in clarifying social work practice' in Compton, B R and Galaway, B (eds) *Social Work Processes* London, The Dorsey Press.

Graham, M (1999) 'The African-centred worldview: developing a paradigm for social work' *British Journal of Social Work* 29(2), pp 252–67.

Graham, M (2000) 'Honouring social work principles-exploring the connections between anti-racist social work and African-centred worldviews' *Social Work Education* 19(5) pp423–36

Graham, M (2001) 'The miseducation of black children in the British educational system, toward an African-centred orientation to knowledge' in Majors, R *Educating Our Black children: New directions and radical approaches* London, Routledge Falmer Press

Graham, M (2002) 'Creating Spaces: exploring the role of cultural knowledge as a source of empowerment in models of social welfare in black communities' Vol 32(1) pp 35-49 *British Journal of Social Work*

Grant, M (1833) Speech reported in *Manchester Courier* 20 April, quoted in Royston Pike, E (1966) *Human Documents of the Industrial Revolution*, London, George Allen & Unwin.

Greenwood, J (1993) quoted in *The Independent*, 28 August and 19 November.

Gutierrez, L (1997) 'Multicultural community organising' in Reisch, M and Gambrill, E (eds) *Social Work in the 21st Century* Thousand Oaks, CA, Pine Forge Press.

Gutierrez, L and Nagda, B (1996) 'The multicultural imperative for human service organisations' in Raffoul, P and McNeece, A (eds) *Future Issues for Social Work Practice* Boston: MA, Allyn & Bacon.

Gyekye, K (1995) *An Essay on African Philosophical Thought* Philadelphia, PA, Temple University Press

Hall, C (1996) 'Histories, empires and the post-colonial moment' in Chambers, I and Curti, L (eds) *The Post-colonial Question, Common Skies, Divided Horizons* London, Routledge.

Hall, S *et al.* (1982) *The Empire Strikes Back* Centre for Contemporary Cultural Studies, London, Hutchinson.

Hall, S and Gieben, B (eds) (1992) *Formations of Modernity* Oxford, Basil Blackwell.

Hardiman, R and Jackson, B (1997) National Conference on Race in Higher Education. San Antonio, Texas

Harding, S and Hintikka, M B (eds) , (1983) *Discovering reality: Feminist perspectives on epistemology, metaphysics, methodology, and philosophy of science* Dordrecht, Holland, Reidel.

Harding, S (1991) *Whose Science? Whose Knowledge? Thinking from Women's Lives* Milton Keynes, Open University Press.

Harris, N (1992) 'A philosophical basis for an Afrocentric orientation' *The Western Journal of Black Studies* 16(3), pp 154–59.

Harris, V (1991) 'Values of Social Work in the Context of British Society in Conflict with Anti-racism' CD Project Steering Group (eds) *Setting the Context for Change* London CCETSW.

Hartman, A (1990) 'Many Ways of Knowing' *Social Work* 35(1), pp 3–4.

Hartman, A (1994a) 'Setting the theme: Many Ways of Knowing' in Sherman, E and Reid, W (eds) *Qualitative Research in Social Work* New York, Columbia University Press.

Hartman, A (1994b) 'Social Work Practice' in Reamer, F (ed.) *The Foundations of Social Work Knowledge* New York, Columbia University Press.

Harvey, A and Rauch, J (1997) 'A comprehensive Afrocentric rites of passage programme for black male adolescents' *Health and Social Work* 22(1) pp 30–7.

Heasman, K (1962) *Evangelicals in Action* London, Bles.

Hegel, G (1956) *The Philosophy of History* (with an introduction by Friedrich, C J) New York, Dover.

Heineman, M (1981) 'The obsolete imperative in social work research' *Social Science Review* 55, pp 343–57.

Hendrick, H (1994) *Child Welfare: England 1872–1989* London, Routledge, Kegan Paul.

Herskovits, M (1958), *The Myth of the Negro Past* Boston, MA, Beacon Press.

Hill, P (1992) *Coming of Age: African American Male Rites of Passage* Chicago, IL, African Images.

Hill, P (1998) *The Journey, (Adolescent Rites of Passage) Youth Workbook* Cleveland, OH, The National Rites of Passage Institute, 2749 Woodhill Road, Cleveland, Ohio 44104.

Hill, R (1971) *The Strengths of Black Families* New York, National Urban League.

Hill, R (1972) *The Strengths of Black Families*, New York, Emerson Hall.

Hill-Collins, P (1991) *Black Feminist Thought: Knowledge, consciousness and the politics of empowerment* New York, Routledge.

Holdstock, T (2000) *Re-examining Pyschology Critical Perspectives and African Insights* London, Routledge.

Holloway, J (ed.) (1990) *Africanisms in American Culture* Bloomington, Indiana University Press.

Hooks, b (1984) *Feminist Theory: From margin to center* Boston, MA, South End Press.

Hooks, b (1996) 'Postmodern blackness' in Truett Anderson, W (ed.) *The Fontana Postmodern Reader* London, Fontana Press.

Howe, D (1997) 'Relating theory to practice' in Davies, M (ed.) *The Blackwell Companion to Social Work* Oxford, Basil Blackwell.

Huggins, N (1990) *Black Odyssey* New York, Vintage Books.

Hume, D (1748) *Essays Moral and Political* (rev. edn) reprinted in Eze, E (ed.) (1997) *Race and the Enlightenment* Oxford, Basil Blackwell.

Humphries, B (1995) *Understanding Research* Milton Keynes, Bucks, Open University Press.

Humphries, B (1997) 'Reading social work: competing discourses in the Rules and Requirements for the Diploma in Social Work' *British Journal of Social Work* 27(5) pp 641–58.

Hunter, D (1983) 'The rhetorical challenge of Afro-centricity' *Western Journal of Black Studies* 7(4) pp 239–43.

Ince, L (1999) 'Preparing young black people for leaving care' in Barn, R (ed.) *Working with Black Children and Adolescents in Need* London, British Agencies for Adoption and Fostering.

John, G (1999) 'The case for a nil exclusions policy: redefining and delivering school students' "entitlement"' Public Lecture, London, WGARCR.

Jones, C (1996) 'Anti-intellectualism and the peculiarities of British social work education' in Parton, N (ed.) *Social Theory, Social Change and Social Work* London, Routledge.

Jones, K (1994) *The Making of Social Policy in Britain, 1830–1990* London, Routlege & Kegan Paul.

Jordan, B (1997) 'Social work and society' in Davies, M (ed.) *Blackwell Companion to Social Work* Oxford, Basil Blackwell.

Kant, I (1775) 'On the different races of man, in *This is Race* (ed E W Count) New York, Henry Schuman, 1950.

Karenga, M (1990a) *The Book of Coming Forth by Day, The Ethics of the Declarations of Innocence, Translation and Commentary* Los Angeles, CA: University of Sankore Press.

Karenga, M (1990b) 'Towards a sociology of Maatian ethics: literature and contex', in Karenga, M (ed.) *Reconstructing Kemetic Culture: papers, perspectives, projects* Los Angeles, University of Sankore Press.

Karenga, M (1993) *Introduction to Black Studies* (2nd edn) Los Angeles, CA, University of Sankore Press.

Karenga, M (1994) 'Maat the moral ideal in ancient Egypt: a study of classical African ethics' Volume 1, unpublished PhD dissertation, University of California.

Karenga, M (1997) *Kwanzaa: A celebration of family, community and culture* Los Angeles, CA, University of Sankore Press

Karenga, M (2000) Internet Source Web site for US organisation.

Keita, L (1990) 'Contemporary African philosophy: the search for a method' in Oruka, H (ed.) *Sage Philosophy Indigenious Thinkers and Modern Debate on African Philosophy* New York, E J Brill.

Keita, L (1994) 'Pearce's African philosophy and the sociological thesis, a response' *Philosophy of the Social Sciences* 24(2) pp 192–203.

Keller, E F (1985) *Reflections on Gender and Science* New Haven, CT, Yale University Press.

Kendall, J (1985) *The Origins of Modern Feminism: Women in Britain, France, and the United States, 1780-1860*, London, Macmillan.

Kincheloe, J and Steinberg, S (1997) *Changing Multiculturalism* Buckingham, Open University Press.

King, A (1994) 'An Afrocentric cultural awareness program for incarcerated African-American males' *Journal of Multicultural Social Work*, 3(4), pp. 17–28.

King, W (1995) *Stolen Childhood, slave youth in 19th century America* Bloomington, IN, Indiana University Press.

Kuhn, T S (1970) *The Structure of Scientific Revolutions* Chicago, IL, University of Chicago Press.

References

Leeds Freedmen's Aid Society (1865) 'A plea for the Perishing', pamphlet, Leeds, John Rylands Library Pamphlets, Manchester quoted in Bolt, C (1971) *Victorian Attitudes to Race* London, Routledge & Kegan Paul.

Lee, J (1994) *The Empowerment Approach to Social Work Practice* New York, Columbia University Press.

Lees, L H (1998) *The Solidarities of Strangers: the English Poor Laws and the people, 1700–1948* Cambridge, Cambridge University Press.

Leiby, J (1997) 'Social work and social responsibility' in Reisch, M and Gambrill, E (eds.) *Social Work in the 21st Century* Thousand Oaks, CA, Pine Forge Press.

Lennon, K and Whitford, M (eds) (1994) *Knowing the Difference: feminist perspectives in epistemology* London, Routledge.

Lewis, G (2000) 'Discursive histories, the pursuit of multiculturalism and social policy' in Lewis, G and Gewirtz, S and Clarke, J (eds) *Rethinking Social Policy* London Sage Publications and Open University.

Liebow E (1967) *Tally's Corner* Boston, MA, Little, Brown.

Lipsey, M W (1993) 'Theory as method: Small Theories of Treatments' in Sechrest, L B and Scott, A G (eds) *Understanding Causes and Generalising About Them* San Francisco: Jossey-Bass.

Lloyd, G (1984) *The Man of Reason: 'male' and 'female' in Western philosophy* Minneapolis,MN, University of Minnesota Press.

Lorde, A (1984) *Sister Outsider* New York, The Crossing Press.

Lorimer, D (1984) 'Black slaves and English liberty' *Immigrants and Minorities* 3, pp 121–50.

Lorimer, D (1992) 'Black resistance to slavery and racism in eighteenth century England' in (eds) Gundasra, J & Duffield, I, (eds) *Essays on the history of Balcks in Britain* Aldershot, Ashgate.

Lyotard, J (1984) *The Postmodern Condition: A report on knowledge* Manchester, Manchester University Press.

Macdonald, S (1991) *All Equal Under the Act?* London, Race Equality Unit, National Institute of Social Work.

Macey, M and Moxon, E (1996) 'An examination of anti-racist and anti-oppressive theory and practice in social work education' *British Journal of Social Work* 26, pp 297–31.

Mackenzie-Grieve, A (1968) *The Last Years of the English Slave Trade Liverpool 1750–1807* London, Frank Cass.

157

Magdol, E (1977) *A Right to Land: Essays on the Freedman's Community* Westport, CT, Greenwood.

Makosky, V P and Paludi, M A (1990) 'Feminism and women's studies in the academy' in Paludi, M A and Steuernagel, G A (eds) *Foundations for a Feminist Restructuring of the Academic Disciplines* New York, the Haworth Press.

Manning, S (1997) 'The social worker as moral citizen: ethics in action' *Social Work* 42(3) pp 223–30.

Martin, J and Martin, E (1985) *The Helping Tradition in the Black Family and Community,*Silver Spring, MD, National Association of Social Workers.

Martin, J M and Martin, E P (1995) *Social Work and the Black Experience* Washington, DC, National Association of Social Workers Press.

Martinez-Brawley, E (1999) 'Social work, postmoderns and higher Education' *International Social Work* 42(3), pp 333–46.

Maxime J (1993) 'The importance of racial identity for the psychological well-being of Black children' *ACPP Review and Newsletter* 15(4) 173–79.

Mbiti, J (1970) *African Religions and Philosoph*, Garden City, NY, Anchor Books.

McAdoo, H P (1981) *Black Families* Beverly Hills, CA, Sage.

Mercer, K (1984) 'Black communities' experience of psychiatric services', *International Journal of Social Psychiatry* 30(1/2) pp 22–7.

Midgley, C (1992) *Women Against Slavery, the British Campaigns 1780–1870* London, Routledge.

Miller, R (1999) *Holistic education and the emerging culture* Internet source: Transcripts, Ron Miller: Spirituality in Education On-Line.

Minh-ha, Trinh (1989) *Woman, Native, Other: writing postcoloniality and feminism* Bloomington, IN, Indiana University Press.

Mirza, H S and Reay, D (2000) 'Spaces and places of black educational desire: rethinking black supplementary schools as a new social movement' *Sociology* 34(3) pp 521–43.

Mohanty, C (1990) 'On race and voice: challenges of liberal education in the 90s' *Cultural Critique* 14, pp 179–208.

Mowat, C (1961) *The Charity Organisation Society, 1869–1913* London, Methuen.

Moynihan, D (1965) *The Negro Family – the case for national action* Washington, DC Office of Planning and Research, US Department of Labour.

Myers, L (1988) *Understanding an Afrocentric World View: introduction to optimal pyschology* Dubuque, IA, Kendall/Hunt.

Myers, N (1993) 'Servant, Sailor, Tailor, Beggarman: Black survival in white society 1780-1830' *Immigrants and Minorities*, 12(1).

NACRO (1991) *Race and Criminal Justice* NACRO briefing, London, National Association for the Care and Resettlement of Offenders

Naples, N (1999) 'Towards comparative analyses of women's political praxis: explicating multiple dimensions of standpoint epistemology for feminist ethnography', *Women and Politics*, 20(1) pp.29–54.

Nkombe, O and Smet, A J (1978) 'Panorama de la Philosophie Africaine contemporaine' *Recherches Philosophiques Africaines, Vol 3, Melanges de Philosophie Africaine*

Nobles, W (1976) 'Black people in white insanity: an issue for black community mental health' *Journal of Afro American Issues* 4(1) Winter.

Nobles, W (1978) 'Toward an empirical and theoretical framework for defining black families' *Journal of Marriage and Family* November: 679-88.

Nobles, W (1985) *Africanity and the Black Family* Oakland, CA, Black Family Institute.

Nobles, W and Goddard, L (1985) 'Black family life: a theoretical and policy implication literature review' in Harvey, A R (ed.) *The Black Family: An Afrocentric Perspective* New York, United Church of Christ Commission for Racial Justice.

Novak, M (1972) 'Pluralism: a humanistic perspective' *Harvard Encyclopaedia of American ethnic groups*.

Obenga, T (1990) *Ancient Egypt and Black Africa* Chicago, IL, Karnak House.

Obenga, T (1995) *A Lost Tradition: African Philosophy in world history* Philadelphia, PA, Source.

Obonna, P (1996) 'Education of the Black Child' conferences, Rites of Passage programmes, Manchester, Kemetic Guidance Group.

O'Brien, M and Penna, S (1998a) 'Oppositional Postmodern Theory and Welfare Analysis:Anti-Oppressive Practice in a Postmodern Frame', in Carter, J (ed.) *Postmodernism and the Fragmentation of Welfare* London, Routledge.

O'Brien, M and Penna, S (1998b) *Theorising Welfare Enlightenment and Modern Society* London, Sage.

Okundaye, J N, Gray, K and Gray, L B (1999) 'Reimaging field instruction from a spiritually sensitive perspective: an alternative approach' *Social Work* 44(4) pp 371–83.

Oruka, H (1990) *Sage Philosophy: indigenous thinkers and modern debate on African philosophy* New York, E J Brill.

Outlaw, L (1990) 'African philosophy: deconstructive and reconstructive challenges' in Oruka, H (ed.) *Sage Philosophy: indigenous thinkers and modern debate on African philosophy* New York, E J Brill.

Outlaw, L (1996) *Race and Philosophy* New York, Routledge.

Outlaw, L (1998) 'African, African American, Africana Philosophy' in Eze, E (ed.) *African Philosophy An Anthology* Oxford, Basil Blackwell.

Patterson, S (1963) *Dark Strangers* London, Tavistock.

Payne, M (1991) *Modern Social Work Theory: a critical introduction* London, Macmillan.

Pender hughes, E (1989) *Understanding Race, Ethnicity and Power: the key to efficacy in clinical practice* London, Macmillan

Penny, P and Best, F (1988) *The Black Child in the Care System* London, ABSWAP.

Perkin, H (1969) *The Origins of Modern English Society 1780–1880*,London, Routledge & Kegan Paul.

Perkins, U (1985) *Harvesting New Generations: the positive development of black youth* Chicago, IL, Third World Press.

Phillips, M (1982) 'The meaning of separatism' in Ohri, A, Manning, B and Curno P (eds) *Community Work and Racism* London, Routledge & Kegan Paul.

Phoenix, A (1988 'The Afro-Caribbean myth' *New Society* 4March pp 11–14.

Pinderhughes, E (1994) 'Diversity and Populations at Risk: Ethnic Minorities and People of Color' in Reamer, F (ed.) *The Foundations of Social Work Knowledge* New York, Columbia University Press.

Popple, K (1995) *Analysing Community Work, its theory and practice* Buckingham, Open University Press.

Prevatt, B (2000) 'Ethnicity and placement: beginning the debate' *Adoption and Fostering* 24(1) Spring, pp 9–14.

Pryce K (1979) *Endless Pressure: a study of west indian life-styles in Bristol* Handsworth Penguin.

Rainwater, L (1970) *Behind Ghetto Walls: Black families in a Federal Slum* Chicago, IL, Aldine.

Reamer, F (1993) *The Philosophical Foundations of Social Work* New York, Columbia University Press.

Reamer, F (1994) 'Social Work Values and Ethics' in Reamer, F (ed.) *The Foundations of Social Work Knowledge* New York, Columbia University Press.

Reamer, F (1997) 'Ethical issues for social work practice' in Reisch, M and Gambrill, E (eds) *Social Work for the 21st Century* Thousand Oaks, CA, Pine Forge Press.

Reamer, F (1998) 'The evolution of social work ethics', *Social Work* 43(6), pp.488–98.

Richards, D (1980) *Let the Circle be Unbroken: Implications of African Spirituality in the Diaspora* Trenton, NJ, Red Sea Press.

Richmond, M (1917) *Social Diagnosis* New York, Russell Sage Foundation.

Robinson, L (1995) *Psychology for Social Workers, Black Perspectives* London, Routledge.

Rodney, W (1974) *How Europe Underdeveloped Africa* Washington, DC: Howard University Press.

Rhodes, M (1992) 'Social work challenges: the boundaries of ethics' *Families in Society* 73, pp 40–7.

Rooff, M (1972) *A Hundred Years of Family Welfare* London, Michael Joseph.

Roys, P (1993) 'Social Services' in Bhat, A, Carr-Hill, R and Ohri, S (eds) *Britain's Black Population (2nd edn)* Aldershot, Ashgate.

Ryan, T and Walker, R (1993) *Life Story Work* London, British Agencies for Adoption and Fostering

Ryan, W (1971) *Blaming the Victim* New York: Pantheon.

Safoa, The National African and Caribbean Mental Health Network – Charter for Mental Health Services

Said, E W (1979) *Orientalism* New York, Vintage Books.

Semaj, L T (1996) 'Towards a cultural science' in Azibo Daudi Ajani ya (ed.) *African Psychology in Historical Perspective and Related Commentary* Trenton, NJ, Africa World Press.

Schiele, J (1990) 'Organisational theory from an afrocentric perspective', *Journal of Black Studies* 21(2), pp. 145–161

Schiele, J (1994) 'Afrocentricity as an alternative worldview for equality' *Journal of Progressive Human Services* 5(1) pp 5–25.

Schiele, J (1997) 'The contour and meaning of Afrocentric social work' *Journal of Black Studies* 27(6) pp 800–19.

Schiele, J (2000) *Human Services and the Afrocentric Paradigm* New York, Haworth Press.

Scheurich, J and Young, M (1997) 'Coloring epistemologies, are our research epistemologies racially biased?' *Educational Researcher* 26(4) pp 4–16.

Shyllon, F (1974) *Black Slaves in Britain* London, Institute of Race Relations/Oxford University Press.

Shyllon, F (1977a) *Black People in Britain 1555–1833* London, Oxford University Press.

Shyllon, F (1977b) 'Olaudah Equiano, Nigerian abolitionist and 1st national leader an African in Britain' *Journal of African Studies* 7, pp 433–51.

Simon, B Levy (1990) 'Rethinking empowerment' *Journal of Progressive Services*, 1(1) pp 27–39.

Skellington, R and Morris P (1992) *Race in Modern Britain Today* Newbury Park, CA, Sage.

Small J (1982) 'New Black Families' *Adoption and Fostering* 6(3) pp 35–9.

Small J (1984) 'The Crisis in Adoption' *International Journal of Social Psychiatry* 30(1/2) Spring.

Small, S (1994) *Racialised Barriers, The Black Experience in the United States and England in the 1980s* London, Routledge.

Social Exclusion Unit (1998) *Truancy and School Exclusion Report* London, HMSO

Solomon, B (1976) *Black Empowerment: social work in oppressed communities* New York, Columbia University Press.

Solomon, B (1987) 'Empowerment: social work in oppressed communities' *Journal of Social Work Practice* May pp 79–91.

Specht, H and Courtney, M (1994) *Unfaithful Angels: how social work has abandoned its mission* New York, Free Press.

Staples, R (1974) *The Black Family: essays and studies* Belmont, CA, Wadsworth.

References

Stanfield, J (1994) 'Ethnic modelling in qualitative research' in Denzin, N and Lincoln, Y S (eds.) *Handbook of Qualitative Research* Thousand Oaks, CA, Sage Publications.

Stanfield, J H (1985) 'The ethnocentric basis of social science knowledge production' *Review of Research in Education* 12, pp 387–415.

Stephan, N (1982) *The Idea of Race in Science* New York, Macmillan.

Stephen Lawrence Inquiry (1999) *Report of an inquiry by Sir William Macpherson of Cluny* (Macpherson Report) London, TSO, Cm 4262.

Stein, I (1974) *Systems Theory, Science and Social Work* Metchen NJ, Scarecrow Press.

Stevens, A (1982) *Archetypes: a natural history of the self* New York, William Morrow.

Stocking, G (1982) *Race, Culture and Evolution* Chicago, IL, University of Chicago Press.

Strickland, S (1994)' Feminism, Postmodernism and Difference' in Lennon, K and Whitford, M (eds) *Knowing the Difference, Feminist Perspectives in Epistemology* London, Routledge.

Stuckey, S (1996) 'Slavery and white America' in Clarke, J H (ed.) *Critical Lessons in Slavery and the Slave trade* Richmond, VA, Native Sun.

Suda, C (1997) 'Street children in Nairobi and the African cultural ideology of kin-based support system: change and challenge' *Child Abuse Review* 6(3) pp 199–217.

Sudbury, J (1997) 'Black women's organisations and the politics of transformation' unpublished thesis, University of Warwick.

Sudbury, J (1998) *Other Kinds of Dreams, Black Women's Organisations and the Politics of Transformation* London, Routledge.

Sullivan, W (1992) 'Reconsidering the environment as a helping resource' in Saleebey, D (ed.) *The Strengths Perspective in Social Work Practice* New York, Longman.

Thomas, A and Sillen, S (1972) *Racism and Psychiatry* Secaucus, NJ, The Citadel Press.

Thompson, N (1993) *Anti-Discriminatory Practice* London, Macmillan.

T'Shaka, O (1995) *Return to the African Mother Principle of Male and Female Equality* Volume 1, Oakland, CA, Pan Afrikan.

Tuhiwai Smith, L (1999) *Decolonising Methodologies Research and Indigenous Peoples* London, Zed Books.

Turner, M (1982) *Slaves and Missionaries: the disintegration of Jamaican slave society, 1787–1834* Urbana, IL, University of Illinois Press.

Turner, F J (1986) 'Theory in social work practice' in Turner, F J (ed) *Social Work Treatment* New York, Free Press.

Verharen, C (1995) 'Afrocentrism and acentrism: a marriage of science and philosophy' *Journal of Black Studies* 26(1), pp 62–76.

Wakefield, J C (1993) 'Is altruism part of human nature? Toward a theoretical foundation for the helping professions' *Social Service Review* 62, pp 187–210.

Wakefield, J C (1996) 'Does social work need the eco-systems perspective? Part 1: Is the perspective useful?' *Social Service Review* 70, pp 1–32.

Walvin, J (1994) 'Black People in Britain' in Tibbs, A (ed.)*Transatlantic Slavery: against Human Dignity* London, HMSO

Walz, T and Ritchie, H (2000) 'Gandhian principles in social work practice: ethics revisited' *Social Work* 45(3) pp 213–17.

Warfield-Coppock, N (1990) *Afrocentric Theory and Applications: adolescent rites of passage* Washington DC, Baobab Associates.

Warfield-Coppock, N (1997) 'The feminine and masculine conceptual framework' in Watts, R and Jagers, R (eds) *Manhood development in urban African-American communities* New York, Haworth Press.

Webb, S and McBeath, G (1989) 'A Political Critique of Kantian Ethics in Social Work' *British Journal of Social Work* 19(6), pp 491–506.

Weick, A (1987) 'Reconceptualising the philosophical perspective of social work' *Social Service Review* 61(2) pp 218-230.

Wells Irme, R (1984) 'The nature of knowledge in social work' *Social Work* 29, 41–5.

West, C (1989) 'Black culture and post-modernism' in Kruger, B and Mariani, P (eds) *Remaking History* Dia Art Foundation, Seattle, WA, Bay Press.

Westgate, C E (1996) 'Spiritual wellness and depression' *Journal of Counselling and Development* 75(1) pp 26–35.

Wilcox, D (1998) 'The Rites of Passage Process for African-American Youth, Perspectives of Eight Elders' unpublished PhD thesis, Ohio, Kent State University.

Williams, C (1987) *The Destruction of Black Civilisations: Great Issues of a Race from 4500 BC to 2000 AD* Chicago, IL, Third World Press.

Williams, C (1999) 'Connecting anti-racist and anti-oppressive theory and practice, retrenchment or reappraisal?' *British Journal of Social Work* 29(2,) pp211–30.

Woodroofe, K (1962) *From Charity to Social Work* , London, Routledge & Kegan Paul.

Worsley, P (1973) *Problems in Modern Society* Harmondsworth, Penguin.

Yeatman, A (1994) *Postmodern Revisionings of the Political* New York, Routledge.

Young, I M (1990) *Justice and the Politics of Difference* Princeton, NJ, Princeton University Press.

Zahan, D (1970) *The Religion, Spirituality and Thought of Traditional Africa* Chicago, University of Chicago Press.